Chinese Cooking in the American Kitchen

CHINESE COOKING IN THE AMERICAN KITCHEN

EVA LEE JEN

KODANSHA INTERNATIONAL LTD.

TOKYO, NEW YORK & SAN FRANCISCO

Distributed in the United States by Kodansha International/USA, Ltd., through Harper & Row, Publishers, Inc., 10 East 53rd Street, New York, New York 10022; in Canada by Fitzhenry & Whiteside Limited, 150 Lesmill Road, Don Mills, Ontario; in Mexico and Central America by HARLA S.A. de C.V., Apartado 30-546, Mexico 4, D.F.; in South America by Harper & Row, International Department; in the United Kingdom by Phaidon Press Ltd., Littlegate House, St. Ebbe's Street, Oxford OX1 1SQ; in Continental Europe by Boxerbooks Inc., Limmatstrasse 111, 8031 Zurich; in Australia and New Zealand by Book Wise (Australia) Pty. Ltd., 104–8 Sussex Street, Sydney 2000; in the Far East by Toppan Company (S) Pty. Ltd., Box 22 Jurong Town Post Office, Jurong, Singapore 22.

Published by Kodansha International Ltd., 2-12-21 Otowa, Bunkyo-ku, Tokyo 112, and Kodansha International/USA, Ltd., 10 East 53rd Street, New York, N.Y. 10022 and 44 Montgomery Street, San Francisco, California 94104. Copyright © 1978 by Kodansha International Ltd. All rights reserved. Printed in the United States of America.

Designed by Sidney Feinberg

LCC 77-94480
ISBN 0-87011-331-3
JBC 1095-2077-786441-2361

78 79 80 81 10 9 8 7 6 5 4 3 2

To D. J. and R.

Contents

Acknowledgments

I am grateful to my friend June Bartnett, whose encouragement and aid in preparing the manuscript helped to bring this book to its completion.

My grateful thanks also go to Dr. Howard Parsons, Mr. and Mrs. Henry Hufschmied, Mrs. Jackie Strobel, and Mr. David Liu.

Introduction

My purpose in writing *Chinese Cooking in the American Kitchen* is to introduce the technique of Chinese cooking with utensils readily accessible in the American home and ingredients available in supermarkets and health-food stores.

Because most Chinese cookbooks give no exact measurements, I have translated, then tested, each recipe many times to determine the exact amount of each ingredient and its available substitute. I have resolved the myth of Chinese cooking and show that one need not use special foods or special utensils to maintain the authentic taste of Chinese dishes.

ABBREVIATIONS

The following abbreviations, in addition to the standard forms, are used in this book:

T. = tablespoon
t. = teaspoon
c. = cup

Chinese Cooking in the American Kitchen

SOME HELPFUL
HINTS

Here are some of the things I have learned from sixteen years of cooking and seven years of teaching Chinese cuisine.

Salt and soy sauce are the basic flavorings for Chinese food. It is advisable to use them conservatively. Keep in mind: 1 scant teaspoon of salt (or 2½ tablespoons of soy sauce) seasons 1 pound of meat.

The best wine for cooking is the one which the cook enjoys drinking the most. To eliminate extra sweet taste and undesirable color, however, stick with dry white wine.

Whenever possible, have butcher cut, grind, or slice as much as possible. Most fish stores will clean and prepare fish the way you want it. This will save you time, work, and most of all, your nerves.

Meat, poultry, and seafood taste better if they have never been frozen. This is especially true with fish. And lobster, crab, and clams have to be cooked alive or right after killing.

Shrimp has a very delicate texture. If it is frozen, overdefrosting may cause loss of its juice. When you are in a hurry, rinse frozen shrimp with cold water in a colander or strainer until it turns soft to the touch. Drain well before using.

Chinese cooking often requires quite a bit of preparation. But a little planning before and some work after food shopping can make cooking for the week a pleasure rather than a chore. Here are some hints:

Cut meat and poultry into desired size and shape. Pack into double plastic bags. Tuck in flap, pat into a square, and label. Freeze, or refrigerate if you plan to use within 24 hours.

Shrimp in the shell should be prepared according to instructions given in recipes. Rinse, drain well. Pack into double sandwich bags, tuck in flap, label, and freeze.

Wrap porkchops, two at a time, in plastic paper, before sealing the whole bundle in plastic bag—makes it much easier to defrost.

Whenever possible, buy fresh fish, live lobster, and crab the same day you plan to cook it.

Ground meats can be mixed with required ingredients and seasonings, then packaged and frozen.

Canned bamboo shoots and water chestnuts keep well in a jar filled with cold water. Screw on lid and refrigerate on top shelf. Change water every week.

Eggplant, yams or sweet potatoes, potatoes, onions, and garlic stay fresh longest in partially sealed plastic bags within a brown bag in a cool place. Never refrigerate eggplant, yams, or sweet potatoes: excessive cold turns them black inside.

Vegetables, except very delicate ones such as iceberg lettuce, can be washed and cut into desired sizes, sealed in plastic bags, and refrigerated for up to 48 hours.

There are three ways to store ginger roots: (1) Bury in white sand. Place in cool place. (2) Pare skin, wash, cut into desired slices. Place in jar. Cover with dry white wine and screw on top. Refrigerate. (3) Pack ginger slices in double plastic bags and freeze. Take out of freezer just before using—if you defrost, you will lose the juice.

Dry mushrooms keep well at room temperature, but be sure to seal tight in plastic bag against humidity.

In reheating leftover foods, for best results, treat different types of cooking with different methods:

To reheat deep-fried foods: Heat fryer to medium-high temperature. Arrange food evenly over bottom of pan. Cover and lower heat to medium. Brown 2–3 minutes. Turn and brown other side.

To reheat quick-fried foods: Heat pan to medium-high temperature. Cover and heat only to hot. Do not boil—boiling will toughen meats and cause green vegetables to change color.

To reheat roasted poultry: Cut into about 1-by-2-inch pieces, if necessary. Heat frying pan to medium-high temperature. Add 1–1½ T. vegetable oil. Swirl to coat bottom of pan. Place poultry bone side down first. Cover and brown 3–4 minutes. Turn and brown skin side.

To reheat steamed or boiled stuffed biscuits or dumplings: Heat frying pan to medium-high temperature. Add 1½ T. vegetable oil, swirl to coat bottom, and heat a few seconds. Arrange biscuits around edge of pan. Brown 1–2 minutes. Pour ¼ c. water into center of pan. Cover and cook until water evaporates completely (about 5 minutes).

To reheat soup with green vegetables: Heat soup in covered saucepan over medium-high temperature just to hot. Remove from heat and cover partially if not served immediately.

Caution: When adding oil to a hot skillet, do so with care— the oil may spatter.

COOKING
TERMS

BOILING: Start root vegetables, bamboo shoots, eggs, with cold water; start everything else with boiling water.

BROWNING: Cook seasonings, meat, vegetables, in hot oil until they turn partially brown, to bring out natural fragrance.

DEEP FRYING: For best results, use electric fryer. Oil should be deep enough to immerse foods to be deep fried; preheat oil to the required temperature before dropping food into it. Underheated oil tends to soak into food and make it greasy. Overheated oil browns the outside too quickly while the inside is not cooked.

QUICK FRYING, OR STIR FRYING: One of the unique and most often used Chinese cooking techniques. "Quick" means the food is cooked over high heat, in smoking hot oil, in a very short time (usually 1 minute or less). To assure success, you need a proper-size saucepan—a large pot (3½ qt. or 4 qt.) or a medium pot (2 qt. or 3 qt.). The heavier the weight, the better. Never use an aluminum pot for quick frying. Preheat empty pan to high temperature before adding oil, to accumulate enough heat in pan and to prevent food from sticking.

MARINATING: Food is marinated before cooking for the same reason as it is coated with flour, egg, and bread crumbs before deep frying: to protect it from direct contact with oil. It also allows marinade to soak into food to enhance flavor. There are two basic groups of marinade: light marinade (cornstarch, wine, salt, with or without egg white) and dark marinade (cornstarch, soy sauce, with or without wine).

ROASTING: A well-roasted chicken or duck (the Chinese way) should be crisp on the outside and tender and juicy inside. To reach such satisfying results, the skin must be dried to be tight and dry to the touch but without wrinkles. Overdried skin means partially dried meat. Roast at moderate temperature until meat is about done. Devote last 15 minutes of roasting to high temperature to give skin a final touch of browning and crispness.

STEAMING: In regular steamer, be sure water in the bottom pan is 2 to 4 inches deep, so it won't dry too soon or touch food to be steamed while boiling. Place food in steamer after water comes to a boil. To make your own steamer, place 1½-qt. Corning Ware or other heatproof cooking dish in 6-qt. pan. Fill inside and outside of dish with 2 inches of water. Put food in aluminum or foil tray and place on top of dish. Cover pan, and you have a one-layer steamer.

ABOUT TEA

Chinese drink tea as much and as often as Americans consume coffee and soft drinks.

There are basically three kinds of tea: unfermented green tea, semifermented oolong tea, and fermented black tea.

Each kind of tea is sorted into many brands, according to the location of the plant, the time of picking, the type of leaf, and the techniques involved in processing.

To walk into a Chinese tea store is like walking into a Chinese pharmacy. It takes an expert not to get lost among the more than one hundred specified names. Most Chinese tea drinkers, especially beginners, stick to unfermented or semifermented teas for their mild refreshing taste. Green tea scented with dry jasmine or chrysanthemums is among the most popular.

Chinese teas are almost always served hot and plain. Tea is served any time and all the time, especially during and after meals. It refreshes the spirit as well as the palate. It also helps in digesting food.

To serve tea to 1 or 2 people, place ½ t. tea in 8-oz. tall heatproof glass. Add boiling water to about 1 inch from the top. Wait until the tea leaves sink to the bottom (about 3 minutes). As you drink, refill with boiling water. Green tea will turn darker and milder after the first glass. If a smaller or shallower glass or cup is used, after adding boiling water to tea, cover glass and wait 2–3 minutes, to give sufficient heat to brew the tea.

For 4–6 servings, place 2–3 t. tea leaves in teapot. Add boiling water. Cover and let stand about 5 minutes (or until leaves sink to the bottom).

SUGGESTED
MENUS

In planning a menu, take the following factors into consideration before consulting the cookbook:

The season or weather: A stew or hot pot cookery is always heartwarming in snowy winter, even though the house is heated. A cold platter is always refreshing served in hot weather. It is also wise to plan your meals according to what foods are in season. They are normally fresher, abundant and reasonable in price.

Budget: A pound of shrimp can be made into an appetizer with cocktails; or, under a tight budget, a pound of shrimp plus some vegetables and a little work can stuff enough Chinese dumplings to feed 4-6 people happily.

Total working time: Some dishes (such as a stew or roast) take longer cooking time but require very little manual work. Others (such as quick-fried dishes) can be cooked within minutes but require more preparation. It is wise not to plan a menu which involves too many work-consuming dishes.

In the following chart, the main dish is listed in alphabetical order with ideas for foods which are compatible for a meal for 4 people. Of course the dishes are interchangeable. You might want almond curd delight for dessert with fish, or liver and spinach soup with roast chuck. Although the alphabetical order is of the main dish, the chart is made in the order one enjoys eating: soup, appetizer, main dish, vegetable/salad, starch food, dessert.

Soup	Appetizer	Main Dish	Vegetable or Salad	Starch	Dessert
Egg Drop		Beef & Cabbage	Pickled Cabbage	Cooked Rice	Sherbet and Mandarin Oranges
Wonton	Fancy Shrimp Cocktail	Beef & Broccoli		Cooked Rice	Golden Coins
Beef Shank & Tomato	Shrimp Rolls	Boiled Fresh Flounder	Bacon-flavored Spinach	Cooked Rice	Golden Coins
Egg Drop	Cucumber Relish	Chicken & Cashews		Cooked Rice	Golden Coins
Beef Shank & Tomato	Sour & Spicy Cabbage	Chinese Dumplings			Almond Delight
Sour & Spicy		Egg Rolls—Beef or Shrimp Stuffing	Vegetable Salad		Almond Delight
Cream of Corn	Stuffed Mushrooms	Fast-stewed Chicken	Pickled Cabbage	Double-layer Pancakes	Sherbet and Mandarin Oranges
Chicken		Flank Steak & Green Peppers	Quick-fried Chinese Cabbage	Cooked Rice	Sesame Crisp
Clam	Shrimp Rolls	Flank Steak & Green Peppers		Cooked Rice	Sherbet and Mandarin Oranges
Stuffed Cucumber		Ginger-flavored Beef Supreme	Quick-fried Chinese Cabbage	Cooked Rice	Almond Delight
Egg Drop	Fancy Shrimp Cocktail	Golden-browned Chicken Fillet	Pickled Cabbage	Cooked Rice	Sherbet and Mandarin Oranges
Stuffed Cucumber		Golden Brown Fish Fillet with Bacon	Vegetable Salad	Cooked Rice	Almond Delight

Soup	Appetizer	Main Dish	Vegetable or Salad	Starch	Dessert
		Hot Pot Cookery			Sesame Crisp
Cream of Corn	Hot Cucumber Relish	Jellied Chicken Mold		Cooked Rice	Sesame Crisp
Egg Drop	Shrimp Rolls	Lobster Cantonese	Vegetable Salad	Cooked Rice	Sherbet and Mandarin Oranges
Liver & Spinach	Sour & Spicy Cabbage	Meatball Daisy		Cooked Rice	Almond Cookies
Beef Shank & Tomato		Mu-hsu Pork— Spring Roll Stuffing #2		Double-layer Pancakes	Sherbet and Mandarin Oranges
Cream of Corn	Cucumber Relish	Peppercorn Chicken Parts	Vegetable Salad	Cooked Rice	Sesame Crisp
Wonton		Peppercorn-flavored Fresh Fish	Quick-fried Chinese Cabbage	Cooked Rice	Sherbet and Mandarin Oranges
Scallion-flavored Beef	Chicken Crisp	Quick-stewed Fish Steaks		Cooked Rice	Sesame Crisp
	Chicken Crisp	Quick-stewed Pork Butt & String Beans	Pickled Cabbage (6–7 days old)	Cooked Rice	Sesame Crisp
Beef Shank & Tomato	Fancy Shrimp Cocktail	Roast Duck— Peking Style	Vegetable Salad	Double-layer Pancakes	Almond Delight
Chinese Cabbage & Ham	Egg Rolls—Beef Stuffing	Sautéed Shrimp	Quick-fried Broccoli	Cooked Rice	Sherbet and Mandarin Oranges

Sour & Spicy		Scallop Pancakes	Quick-fried Broccoli	Cooked Rice	Sherbet and Mandarin Oranges
Stuffed Cucumber		Golden Brown Shrimp & Cabbage Patties	Vegetable Salad	Cooked Rice	Golden Coins
Wonton	Sour & Spicy Cabbage	Shrimp & Sweet Peas		Cooked Rice	Golden Coins
Clam	Mini Beef Skewers	Shrimp & Vegetables		Cooked Rice	Sesame Crisp
Stuffed Cucumber	Hot Cucumber Relish	Sweet & Sour Pork		Cooked Rice	Sesame Crisp
Chinese Cabbage & Ham	Shrimp Toast	Sweet & Sour Striped Bass	Pickled Cabbage	Cooked Rice	Sesame Crisp
Sour & Spicy		Turkey Roll		Steamed Buns or Bread	Almond Delight
Egg Drop	Golden Browned Chicken Wings	Twice-cooked Beef Shank	Pickled Cabbage (2 days old)	Cooked Rice or Spaghetti	Sherbet and Mandarin Oranges
Egg Drop	Sweet & Sour Shrimp	Twice-cooked Chicken	Pickled Cabbage (2 days old)	Cooked Rice	Almond Cookies

SOUPS

BEEF SHANK AND TOMATO SOUP

Serves 6-8

Two 1¼-inch-thick beef shanks, or 1 chuck steak (about 1 lb.), cut into 1¼-inch cubes, bone and all

2 large, ripe, firm tomatoes (about 1 lb.), quartered

3 scallions, cut into 1½-inch lengths

2 thick slices ginger root, minced, or 1 t. ginger powder

4-5 dry mushrooms, softened in warm water, rinsed, and drained

1 small bundle cellophane noodles softened in hot water, drained, or 1 c. cooked egg noodles

2 t. salt

¼ t. black pepper

few drops sesame oil

Bring 1 qt. water to a boil in pressure cooker. Add beef, tomato, scallions, ginger, and mushrooms. Cover and cook under 10 lbs. pressure for 45 minutes. Remove from burner. Set pot aside for 10 minutes. Rinse under cold water and release pressure. (If regular covered pot is used, simmer soup 3-3½ hours, or until beef is tender.)

Bring soup to another boil without pressure. Stir in remaining ingredients.

CHICKEN SOUP

Serves 6-8

½ young chicken, or chicken parts
  (about ¾ lb.)
5-6 dry mushrooms, rinsed
2 scallions, cut into 2-inch lengths
2 thin slices ginger root or 1 t.
  ginger powder
2 T. dry white wine

2 t. salt
1 small bundle cellophane
  noodles, softened in hot water,
  drained, or 1 c. cooked egg
  noodles
½ t. white pepper
few drops sesame oil (optional)

In pressure cooker, bring 1 qt. water to a boil. Put in chicken and cook under 10 lbs. pressure for 20 minutes. Cool cooker for 10 minutes. Rinse under cold water. Release pressure. (If regular covered pot is used, simmer 1½-2 hours, or until chicken is tender.)

Add mushrooms, scallions, ginger, wine, and salt. Cook without pressure for 10 minutes.

Add noodles to soup. Sprinkle with pepper, and sesame oil if you like.

CHINESE CABBAGE AND HAM SOUP

Serves 4-6

1 T. vegetable oil
2 oz. Virginia ham or smoked
  pork butt, cut into thin pieces
  (about 1 by 1 inch)

4 Chinese cabbage leaves (tender
  ivory-colored only), cut
  crosswise into 1½-inch lengths,
  stem and all
1 qt. chicken broth
¾ t. salt
2 scallions, coarsely chopped

Heat medium-size saucepan to medium-high temperature. Add oil. Heat for a few seconds. Add ham. Quick-fry for about ½ minute. Stir in cabbage. Turn heat to high. Quick-fry until cabbage changes color (about 2 minutes).

Pour chicken broth into pan. Cover and bring to a boil. Lower heat to medium and simmer 2–3 minutes. Add salt. Sprinkle scallions over soup before serving.

CLAM SOUP

Serves 4

1 t. minced ginger root or ½ t. ginger powder
1¼ t. salt (or to taste)

12 live small little-neck clams, brushed under running water, soaked in water for 4–6 hours
¼ t. sesame oil

Bring 1 qt. water to a boil. Add ginger and salt. Put in clams and return water to a boil. Cover until clams open (about 2 minutes). Discard any clams that don't open.

Add sesame oil and divide into 4 bowls, shells and all.

CREAM OF CORN SOUP

Serves 8–10

16-oz. can creamed corn
¼ t. salt
2 T. cornstarch dissolved in ¼ c. water
2 T. minced Virginia ham or pastrami

1 qt. chicken broth
1 large egg white, slightly beaten
¼ t. white or black pepper

Combine corn, salt, cornstarch mixture, ham or pastrami, and chicken broth in pot. Bring to a rolling boil.

Hold egg white bowl 12 inches above pot. Slowly pour egg white into soup. Gently stir in one direction a few times. Remove pot from heat. Sprinkle soup with pepper.

EGG DROP SOUP

Serves 6–8

1 qt. chicken or pork broth
1 small bunch watercress or 10–12
  fresh spinach leaves, cut
  crosswise in half
1 small pkg. cellophane noodles
  softened in hot water, drained,
  or 1 cup cooked egg noodles

1 large egg, slightly beaten with
  ¼ t. salt
¾ t. salt
1–2 scallions, chopped
¼ t. black pepper
few drops sesame oil (optional)

Bring broth to a boil. Add watercress or spinach and noodles.
Bring soup to another boil. Slowly pour egg mixture into boiling soup, holding egg container about 12 inches above pot. Stir in salt.
Remove pot from heat. Gently stir remaining ingredients into soup.

LIVER AND SPINACH SOUP

Serves 6–8

1½ T. soy sauce
1 t. dry white wine
1 t. cornstarch
½ lb. half-frozen chicken or pork
  liver, sliced into ⅛-inch pieces
1 qt. chicken broth

about 12 fresh spinach leaves,
  rinsed, drained, broken
  crosswise in halves (discard ⅓
  inch from end of stem)
1 T. chopped scallions
½ t. minced ginger root or ½ t.
  ginger powder
½ t. black pepper
few drops sesame oil (optional)

Combine soy sauce, wine, and cornstarch, and marinate liver for 15 minutes.
Bring chicken broth to a boil. Add spinach and bring to another boil. Gradually drop liver into boiling broth. Stir gently and bring to another boil. Remove pot from heat, stir in remaining ingredients, heat, and serve.

OXTAIL AND TOMATO SOUP

Serves 8

1–1¼ lb. oxtails, cut into about
    1½-inch lengths
3 large ripe tomatoes, quartered
3 scallions, cut crosswise in half

3 thin slices ginger root or 2 t.
    ginger powder
1 t. white or black pepper
2 t. salt (or to taste)

In pressure cooker, bring 1 qt. water to boil. Add oxtails. Bring to another rolling boil. Drain and rinse oxtails and cooker with hot tap water. Add 1 qt. boiling water to pressure cooker. Cook oxtails under 10 lbs. pressure for 35 minutes. Cool cooker 10 minutes. Rinse under cold water. Release pressure. (If using a regular pot, simmer oxtails for 3 hours.)

Add remaining ingredients to cooker. Cook covered but without pressure for 15 minutes, or until tomato is tender.

OYSTER AND SPINACH SOUP

Serves 6

1 qt. chicken broth
⅓ c. flour
8 oz. fresh oysters, rinsed and
    drained

8–10 spinach leaves or 1 small
    bundle watercress, broken in
    halves, rinsed, and drained
1 T. chopped scallions
¼ t. white pepper

Bring broth to a boil.

Place flour in plastic bag. Add oysters, and shake bag back and forth until they are coated with flour.

Drop oysters, a few at a time, into boiling broth. Add spinach or watercress and bring to another boil. Remove from heat. Sprinkle with scallions and pepper.

WONTON SOUP

Serves 8

This soup may be served with a garnish of 1 T. chopped scallions, ¼ t. sesame oil, and ¼ t. black pepper, if preferred.

6 oz. cleaned shrimp, chopped
2 scallions, chopped
2 T. dry white wine
½ t. salt
1 large egg white
1 c. ground pork
⅓ c. water chestnuts, chopped

½ t. minced ginger root or ½ t. ginger powder
1 T. soy sauce
1 T. cornstarch
32 wonton skins (see p. 109)
1 T. cornstarch, mixed in ¼ c. water
1 qt. chicken broth

Mix all ingredients except wonton wrappers, cornstarch mixture, and broth. Stir in one direction until sticky.

Place ½ t. of stuffing near the corner of wonton skin. Roll that corner toward the opposite corner, with filling inside. Brush the two side corners with cornstarch mixture. Overlap corners.

Bring large pot of salted water to a boil. Drop in the wontons, one by one; bring to another boil.

Add ⅔ c. water. Bring to another boil. Drain wontons.

Bring chicken broth to a boil. Add cooked wontons, and serve.

SCALLION-FLAVORED BEEF SOUP

Serves 4–6

½ T. soy sauce
1½ t. cornstarch
½ T. dry white wine
¼ lb. flank steak or other lean
    cut, cut lengthwise in halves,
    then cut crosswise into about
    ⅛-inch-thick pieces
2 T. vegetable oil
1 t. minced ginger root or ½ t.
    ginger powder

3 dry mushrooms, softened in
    warm water, stems removed,
    caps cut into thin slices, or 6–8
    medium-size fresh mushrooms,
    cut into thin slices
¼ c. bamboo shoot slices
1 qt. chicken broth
2 scallions, coarsely chopped
few drops sesame oil (optional)
¼ t. white or black pepper

Combine soy sauce, cornstarch, and wine, and marinate beef for 15 to 30 minutes.

Heat deep pot to high temperature. Add oil, and heat for a few seconds. Stir in beef and quick-fry until three-fourths of meat changes color (less than ½ minute). Scoop up beef. Set aside.

Stir in ginger, mushrooms, and bamboo shoots. Quick-fry for about ½ minute. Add chicken broth and bring to a boil. Return beef to pot. Stir. Sprinkle with scallions, add sesame oil if you like, top with pepper, and serve.

SOUP FU YONG

Serves 6–8

1 T. vegetable oil
2 slices bacon, cut into 1-inch
    lengths
1 qt. chicken broth
2 medium-size ripe tomatoes, each
    cut into 8 pieces

2 T. cornstarch, dissolved in ½ c.
    water with ½ t. salt
1 small bundle watercress or
    10–12 fresh spinach leaves,
    broken crosswise in half
1 large egg, slightly beaten

Heat deep pot to medium-high temperature. Add oil. Brown bacon until crisp. Pour in chicken broth and bring to a boil.

Add tomato and cook until tender (about 10 minutes). Stir in cornstarch mixture. Turn heat to high. Bring broth to a rolling boil. Add watercress or spinach. Bring to another boil.

Slowly pour egg, from a height of at least 12 inches above pot, into soup. Give soup one gentle stir—just to mix without making soup cloudy.

SOUR AND SPICY SOUP

Serves 8–10

This soup can be served without vinegar and pepper, if one prefers. Individual servings of sour and hot soup can be made by adding ½ T. vinegar and ¼ t. pepper to *each cup* of soup.

¼ c. lean thin pork strips (1 inch long)

¼ c. flour

6 c. chicken or pork broth

1 t. salt

1 c. shredded Chinese cabbage or other cabbage or celery

2–3 scallions, cut into 1-inch strips

1 t. minced ginger root or ½ t. ginger powder

½ c. shredded bamboo shoots

5–6 dry mushrooms, softened in warm water, stems removed, caps cut into strips

⅓ c. cornstarch, dissolved in ½ c. water

1 large egg, slightly beaten with ¼ t. salt

few drops sesame oil

⅓ c. cider vinegar

2 T. white pepper

Mix pork strips with flour until well coated. Discard excess flour. Bring broth to a boil and stir in salt, cabbage or celery, scallions, ginger, bamboo shoots, and mushrooms. Cook 1 minute. Stir in cornstarch mixture. Cook until soup thickens (about 1 minute).

Slowly pour egg into soup. Stir *once.*

Stir pork into soup and simmer over low heat for 10 minutes. Add sesame oil, vinegar, and pepper.

STUFFED CUCUMBER SOUP

Serves 4–6

1 c. ground pork or beef
½ t. salt
1 T. dry white wine
1 t. cornstarch
1 t. onion powder
1 large egg white or 1 medium
   egg

2 large, slim, firm cucumbers,
   partially pared
1 qt. chicken or pork broth
2 scallions, chopped
½ t. minced ginger root or ½ t.
   ginger powder
few drops sesame oil (optional)

Combine meat, salt, wine, cornstarch, onion powder, and egg. Stir and mix in one direction until sticky.

Cut cucumbers crosswise into halves. Scoop out seeds with thin serrated knife. Stuff each half with one-fourth of stuffing. Then cut each into 5–6 stuffed rings. Run a toothpick through middle of "ring" to secure stuffing.

Pour chicken broth into pot. Place stuffed cucumbers into *cold* broth. Turn heat to medium-high. Cover. Bring soup to a boil. Sprinkle scallions and ginger into soup. Add sesame oil if you wish. Serve warm.

APPETIZERS

ANTS ON THE TREES

Serves 4 as appetizer

For substitutes for cellophane noodles, see p. 109.

2 T. vegetable oil
1 c. (tightly packed) ground pork or ground round
2 scallions, chopped
1 t. minced ginger root or ½ t. ginger powder
¼ c. chopped water chestnuts
1 T. soy sauce

1 T. cornstarch
⅔ c. chicken broth
1 qt. vegetable oil for deep frying (or enough to cover bottom of saucepan to 2½ inches)
1 small bundle cellophane noodles (1¼–1½ oz.)

Heat deep pot to high temperature. Add 2 T. oil. Heat for a few seconds. Stir in ground meat, scallions, and ginger. Quick-fry until meat changes color (about 2 minutes). Add water chestnuts.

Combine soy sauce, cornstarch, and broth, and stir mixture into pot. Lower heat to medium-high. Stir and cook for about 2 minutes. Remove from heat. Cover and set aside.

Pour 1 qt. oil into medium-size saucepan. Heat to high temperature over small burner. Separate noodles gently to loosen as much as possible without breaking them. When a piece of noodle dropped

21

into hot oil puffs up immediately, oil is ready. Place cellophane noodles in oil. They will puff up and turn white within 3 seconds. Drain on paper towels. Place noodles on serving dish. Pour sauce over noodles and serve immediately.

CHICKEN CRISP

Serves 6–8 as appetizer

½ c. soy sauce

1 whole anise or 1 t. five-fragrance spice powder

2–3 thin slices ginger root or 1 t. ginger powder

3 scallions, cut lengthwise in halves

⅓ t. brown peppercorns or 1 t. black pepper

2 T. dry white wine

1 marble-size piece rock candy or 1 T. dark-brown sugar

12 chicken drumsticks

2 egg yolks, mixed with 1 T. cold water and ¼ t. salt

1 qt. vegetable oil (or enough to cover bottom of pot to 1½ inches)

In pressure cooker, bring 1 qt. water, soy sauce, anise or spice powder, ginger, scallions, pepper, wine, and rock candy or sugar to a boil. Put in chicken, cover, and cook under 10 lb. pressure for 20 minutes. (If a regular medium-size saucepan is used, add ½ c. more water. Simmer chicken, covered, for 50–60 minutes, or until tender.) Cool for 10 minutes and rinse pot under cold water. Uncover. Drain and air-dry chicken at room temperature 3–4 hours, or longer.

Brush chicken with egg yolk mixture. Heat oil to medium-high temperature in deep pot. Deep-fry chicken until golden brown (8–12 minutes). Serve as finger food.

COCKTAIL BEEF

Serves 8 –10 as appetizer or snack

¼ c. vegetable oil
3–4 thin slices ginger root or 1 t.
   ginger powder
1¼ lb. boneless chuck (or
   boneless shank), fat trimmed,
   meat cut into pieces about 1
   inch long, ½ inch wide, ⅓
   inch thick

2 T. dry white wine
¼ c. soy sauce
1¼ t. sugar
1 whole anise (separated) or ½ T.
   five-fragrance spice powder

Heat medium-size deep pot to high temperature. Add oil. Brown ginger for a few seconds. Stir-fry beef until it changes color (about 2 minutes). Add remaining ingredients. Cover and cook over medium heat for 20–25 minutes (or until only ¼ c. juice is left). Stir occasionally while cooking.

Turn heat up to medium high. Remove cover. Stir and cook until no juice is left (about 10 minutes). Can be served hot or cold.

EGG ROLLS—BEEF STUFFING

Serves 4 for lunch, 10 for appetizer

½ lb. flank steak or other lean
   cut, trimmed
3 scallions, cut into 1½-inch strips
2 t. ginger root strips or 1 t.
   ginger powder
½ c. shredded bamboo shoots
½ c. fresh or canned bean sprouts,
   rinsed, well drained
3–4 dry mushrooms, softened in
   warm water, stems removed,
   caps cut into thin strips

1 large egg
2 T. soy sauce
2 T. dry white wine
1½ T. cornstarch
10 egg roll skins, Shanghai style
   (see p. 107 or 108)
1 T. cornstarch, dissolved in ¼ c.
   water
1 qt. vegetable oil (or enough to
   cover bottom of fryer to 1¼
   inches)

Fillet steak into 3 layers. Cut lengthwise into halves, then cut each half (3 layers) crosswise into strips. Combine with remaining ingredients (except egg roll skins, cornstarch mixture, and oil), and mix well.

Place one-tenth of mixture slightly off the center of each skin. Roll up skin to enclose filling. Tuck in sides neatly. Brush open edge with cornstarch mixture to seal. Place each completed egg roll on platter, sealed edge down.

Let set in refrigerator for 10 minutes. (If made ahead of time, wrap each individually in plastic wrap and freeze. Deep-fry frozen egg rolls until golden brown. They will take a few minutes longer to fry on each side.)

Heat oil to 400°. Deep-fry egg rolls (sealed side down first) 3–4 minutes on each side, or until golden brown. Drain on paper towel. Serve hot.

EGG ROLLS—MINIATURE

Serves 8–10 as appetizer

STUFFING

2 T. vegetable oil

½ lb. ground pork or ground round

1 small carrot, chopped (about ½ c.)

1 medium-size onion, chopped (about ½ c.)

2 T. soy sauce

1 T. cornstarch, dissolved in 2 T. water

Heat medium-size pot to high temperature. Quick-fry meat until it changes color (about 1 minute).

Stir in carrot and onion. Cook 1 minute. Add soy sauce and cornstarch mix. Stir and cook until sauce thickens. Cool to room temperature.

EGG ROLL SKINS   *(Makes 24 five-inch squares)*

1¾ c. sifted flour

1 t. salt

3 T. salad oil

½ c. milk, soured with 1 T. vinegar

Mix all ingredients together until formed into a solid pastry.

Flour a piece of wax paper 12 by 12 inches. (Add flour when necessary to keep dough from sticking to paper.) Pinch off piece of dough the size of a walnut. Roll dough around in flour on paper. Roll dough out with small rolling pin to 3 inches square, turning dough over after each roll. Cover dough with another piece of wax paper. Roll dough to 5 inches square. Set each skin aside on floured wax paper.

TO MAKE MINIATURE EGG ROLLS

1 T. cornstarch, dissolved in ¼ c. water

1 qt. vegetable oil (or enough to cover bottom of pot to 1½ inches)

Place 1 rounded teaspoonful of stuffing near one corner of skin. Fold the corner over stuffing. With fingertips, wet open edges of skin with cornstarch mixture. Fold two side corners toward center. Turn last corner to seal egg roll.

Set aside, sealed side down, on *floured* wax paper for 15–20 minutes before deep frying. (If made ahead of time, freeze individually until hard. Keep frozen in plastic bag. Deep-fry frozen egg rolls right from freezer.)

Heat oil to medium-high temperature (375°). Deep-fry egg rolls until golden brown, turning once. Serve hot.

EGG ROLLS—PORK STUFFING

Serves 8–10 as appetizer

2 T. oil

1 lb. ground pork

1–1¼ lb. Chinese cabbage, shredded, mixed well with ⅔ t. salt, let set 15 minutes

4 scallions, cut into 2-inch lengths, then into strips

1 t. minced ginger root or ½ t. ginger powder

½ c. bamboo shoot strips

4–5 large dry mushroom caps (discard stems), softened in warm water, cut into strips

3–4 t. salt

½ t. black pepper

1½ T. soy sauce

½ t. sesame oil

2 T. cornstarch

20 egg roll skins (see p. 109)

2 T. cornstarch, dissolved in ½ c. water

1 qt. oil (or enough to cover bottom of fryer to 1¼ inches)

Heat deep pan to high temperature. Add 2 T. oil. Heat for a few seconds. Stir in pork and cook until meat changes color (about 2 minutes). Remove pan from heat and cool pork to room temperature. Squeeze juice out of cabbage. Add cabbage, scallions, ginger, bamboo shoots, mushrooms, salt, pepper, soy sauce, sesame oil and 2 T. cornstarch to pork. Mix well.

Place one-twentieth of stuffing slightly off the center of each skin. Roll up skin to enclose filling. Tuck in sides neatly. Brush open edge with cornstarch mixture. Fold and seal. Place each completed egg roll on a platter, sealed edge *down*. (You may make the rolls ahead and freeze them in a plastic bag, then fry them while still frozen.)

Heat oil to 400° (or until a bread cube quickly browns). Deep-fry egg rolls (sealed side down first) 1½–2 minutes on each side, or until golden brown. Drain on paper towel. Serve hot.

EGG ROLLS—SHRIMP STUFFING

Serves 8–10 as appetizer

½ lb. large or medium cleaned shrimp, cut into strips
½ c. shredded bamboo shoots
4 dry mushrooms, caps softened in warm water, cut into strips
2–3 scallions, cut into strips
½ t. minced ginger root or ½ t. ginger powder
2 T. dry white wine
½ T. soy sauce
½ t. salt
1 T. cornstarch
10 egg roll skins, Shanghai style (see p. 107 or 108)
1 T. cornstarch, dissolved in 4 T. water
1 qt. vegetable oil (or enough to cover bottom of frying pan to 1¼ inches)

Combine all ingredients except egg roll skins, cornstarch mixture, and oil, and mix well for 3 minutes.

Place one-tenth of stuffing slightly off the center of each skin. Roll up skin to enclose filling. Tuck in sides neatly. Brush open edge with cornstarch mixture to seal. Place each completed egg roll on a platter, sealed edge *down*.

Let set in refrigerator for 10 minutes. (If made ahead of time, wrap each individually in plastic wrap and freeze. Deep-fry frozen egg rolls until golden brown. They will take a few minutes longer to fry on each side.)

Heat oil to 400°. Deep-fry egg rolls (sealed side down first) 3–4 minutes on each side, or until golden brown. Drain on paper towel. Serve hot.

FANCY SHRIMP COCKTAIL

Serves 8–10 as appetizer

1 lb. medium-size shrimp in shells
1 t. salt
⅓ c. ketchup
1 T. grated horseradish

1 t. garlic powder
½ t. black pepper
3–4 tender lettuce leaves, broken
  into large pieces

Slit shrimp back from head to tail halfway through, devein (keep shells on), rinse, and drain.

Dissolve salt in 1 c. water, to a boil. Add shrimp. Stir and cook until shrimp change color and curl up into almost a full circle (about 2 minutes). Drain and remove shells (except tail) while still hot.

Combine ketchup, horseradish, garlic powder, and pepper, and mix well.

Place a small wine glass in center of a soup dish and place soup dish on top of dinner plate. Fill glass with dip mix. Arrange lettuce around glass. Arrange shrimp around edges of glass and soup dish. Cover shrimp and all with plastic wrap. Refrigerate 2–3 hours. To eat, hold shrimp by the tail and dip into cocktail sauce.

FISH CRISP

Makes 3 cups

A few tablespoons of fish crisp add lots of nutritious flavor to hot cereal, cold sandwiches, grilled cheese, salad, and everything you can think of. Fish crisp stays well 2–3 weeks at room temperature; 3–4 months in refrigerator—if it ever lasts that long.

¼ c. vegetable oil
3 scallions, cut into 1-inch-long
  thin strips
½ t. minced ginger or ½ t. ginger
  powder

Four 6½-oz. cans chunk light tuna
2 T. dry white wine
5 T. soy sauce
2½ T. sugar

Heat 12-inch open fryer to high. Add oil, and heat for a few seconds, until hot. Add scallion, ginger, and tuna. Stir and press with wooden spoon (to flake fish), and cook for about 2 minutes.

Stir in wine, soy sauce, and sugar. Lower heat to medium high. Keep stirring and pressing while cooking for another 30 minutes, or until fish changes color to dark brown.

Cool fish crisp to room temperature. Place in a glass jar with tight screw top.

FOIL-WRAPPED CHICKEN

Serves 8 as appetizer

3 T. soy sauce
2 T. dry white wine
1 t. sugar
⅓ t. white pepper

1 lb. chicken fillet, cut into about 1-by-2-inch pieces
1 qt. vegetable oil (or enough to cover bottom of frying pan to 2 inches)

Combine soy sauce, wine, sugar, and pepper, and marinate chicken for ½ hour, mixing occasionally.

Cut one 4-by-4-inch piece of aluminum foil for each chicken piece. Place a piece of chicken slightly off the center of each square. Fold corner nearest to chicken toward center. Overlap sides. Roll and tuck in last corner so package won't open.

Heat oil to medium high (375°). Deep-fry chicken packages until golden brown (about 3 minutes on each side). Each person unwraps his own chicken package.

FRIED WONTONS

Serves 8–10 as appetizer

6 oz. frozen shrimp, defrosted,
  drained well, chopped
1 c. ground pork
2 scallions, chopped
½ t. minced ginger root or ½ t.
  ginger powder
2 T. dry white wine
1 large egg

⅓ c. chopped water chestnuts
⅔ t. salt
1 T. cornstarch
½ lb. wonton skins (see p. 109)
1 T. cornstarch, dissolved in ¼ c.
  water
1 qt. vegetable oil (or enough to
  cover bottom of pan to 2 inches)

Mix shrimp, pork, scallions, ginger, wine, egg, water chestnuts, salt, and 1 T. cornstarch. Stir in one direction until sticky.

Place ½ t. stuffing near the corner of each wonton skin. Roll that corner toward the opposite corner, with filling inside. Brush the 2 side corners with cornstarch mixture. Overlap corners and press to stick.

Heat oil to medium high (375°). Fry wontons, a dozen or so at a time, until golden brown (1½–2 minutes). Drain on paper towels. Serve with a toothpick inserted in each.

GOLDEN BROWNED CHICKEN WINGS

Serves 8 as appetizer

8 chicken wings (about 2 lb.)
2 T. soy sauce
2 t. sugar
1 t. minced ginger root or ½ t.
  ginger powder

1 T. dry white wine
1 t. five-fragrance spice powder
1 qt. vegetable oil (or enough to
  cover bottom of frying pan to
  1½ inches)

Cut chicken wings at the joint to make 16 pieces (save tips for other use). Combine soy sauce, sugar, ginger, wine, and spice powder, and marinate chicken wings for 2 hours, or overnight in refrigerator.

Drain and dry in colander for 3–4 hours, until skin of chicken is dry to the touch. Turn occasionally while drying.

Heat oil to 375°. Deep-fry chicken until dark brown (allow 5–6 minutes on each side). Drain on paper towels and serve hot.

HOT CUCUMBER RELISH

Serves 8

2 large, slim, firm cucumbers,
  partially pared, cut into halves
  lengthwise, seeds removed
1 t. salt

2 T. vegetable oil
2 garlic cloves, crushed
about 2 t. minced hot red pepper
few drops sesame oil

Divide each cucumber half lengthwise. Then cut into ½-inch pieces. Mix cucumbers with salt. Let stand 1 hour. Drain well.

Heat small saucepan to medium-high temperature. Add oil. Heat oil until very hot (about ½ minute). Brown garlic to a light brown. Remove pot from heat. Stir in red pepper to taste. Slowly pour hot oil mix into cucumbers. Add sesame oil. Cool to room temperature. Refrigerate at least ½ hour before serving. (Relish tastes best when refrigerated overnight.)

LETTUCE ROLLS

Serves 4–8 as appetizer

2 T. vegetable oil
1 c. (tightly packed) ground pork
  or chuck
2 scallions, chopped
½ t. minced ginger root or ⅓ t.
  ginger powder
¼ c. chopped bamboo shoots
3 medium-size dry mushrooms,
  softened in warm water, stems
  discarded, caps chopped

2 T. soy sauce
1 T. cornstarch, dissolved in ½ c.
  water with ¼ t. salt
1 qt. vegetable oil for deep frying
  (or enough to cover bottom of
  saucepan to 2½ inches)
1 small bundle cellophane noodles
  (1¼–1½ oz.)
8 medium-size romaine lettuce
  leaves

Heat medium-size saucepan to high temperature. Add 2 T. oil

and heat for a few seconds. Stir in meat and quick-fry until it changes color (about 2 minutes).

Add scallions, ginger, bamboo shoots, and mushrooms. Quick-fry for 1 minute. Stir in soy sauce and cornstarch mixture. Stir and bring to a boil. Cover and simmer over medium heat for 3 minutes, stirring occasionally. Remove from heat and keep warm.

Heat oil for deep frying in medium-size saucepan on small burner. Gently separate noodles as much as possible without breaking them. When a piece of noodle is dropped into oil and it puffs up immediately, oil is ready. Put in noodles. They should puff up within 3 seconds. Drain on paper towels. Place in serving dish.

Pour meat sauce over noodles just before serving. Cut with pie server into 8 parts. Place lettuce on individual dishes. Place one-eighth of noodles and sauce in the middle of each lettuce leaf. Roll up sides, enclosing stuffing. Eat in hand.

MINI BEEF SKEWERS

Makes 8–10 servings as appetizer

1 lb. flank steak, trimmed
24 water chestnuts, halved
¼ c. soy sauce
1 T. sugar
¼ c. dry white wine

1 t. garlic powder
½ t. ginger powder
1 T. cornstarch
½ t. minced hot red pepper

Cut steak lengthwise into about 3-inch-wide pieces, then cut each piece crosswise into ¼-inch-thick pieces. Wrap each piece of steak around a water chestnut half. Secure with a toothpick. Place in double-layered plastic bags.

Combine remaining ingredients and pour over meat. Hold open end of bags and shake gently to coat each skewer with marinade. Press out air and tie opening. Refrigerate overnight.

Heat broiler. Arrange skewers slightly apart in baking pan. Place pan 3–4 inches below heat. Broil 1½–2 minutes on each side.

ROASTED PORK SPARERIBS

Serves 8–10 as appetizer

3–3½ lbs. pork spareribs (Chinese style preferred)
6 T. soy sauce
2 T. dry white wine
1 t. minced ginger root or ½ t. ginger powder

2 T. sesame seed, crushed, or 1 t. sesame oil
2 T. sugar
2 garlic cloves, minced
1 c. water

Separate spareribs by cutting between bones. Marinate for 3 hours, or overnight in refrigerator, in remaining ingredients. Turn ribs occasionally while marinating.

Arrange ribs in shallow baking pan. Roast in 300–325° oven for 2–2½ hours, or until ribs turn dark brown and tender. Turn and brush ribs with remaining marinade 3–4 times while roasting. Serve warm or cold as finger food.

SHRIMP ROLLS

Serves 8–10 as appetizer

6 oz. cleaned shrimp, chopped
6 oz. ground pork
2 scallions, chopped
7–8 water chestnuts, chopped
1 t. minced ginger root or ½ t. ginger powder
⅔ t. salt
2 t. cornstarch

1 large egg
20 thin slices fresh bread
1 T. cornstarch, dissolved in ⅓ c. water
2 qt. vegetable oil (or enough to cover bottom of frying pan to 1½ inches)

Combine shrimp, pork, scallions, water chestnuts, ginger, salt, 2 t. cornstarch, and egg. Stir and mix in one direction for at least 3 minutes, or until mixture is sticky. (Add 1–2 T. water if mixture appears to be dry and hard to stir.)

Trim crusts off bread, 1 or 2 slices at a time. With rolling pin, roll bread to ⅛ inch thick (or a third of its original thickness). Spread shrimp mix thinly, covering three-fourths of the flattened bread. Gently roll up bread and filling. Seal with cornstarch mix. Place each finished roll with sealed side *down*.

Deep fry in 400° oil until golden brown. Turn rolls *only once*. Drain on paper towel. Cut each roll into 3 pieces; stick a toothpick in each and serve hot.

SHRIMP TOAST

Serves 6–8 as appetizer

¾ lb. cleaned shrimp, chopped
1 T. cornstarch
2 scallions, chopped
7–8 water chestnuts, chopped
¼ c. chopped pork fat or bacon fat
¾ t. salt

½ t. minced ginger root or ½ t. ginger powder
1 large egg
8 thin slices stale white bread (if bread is fresh, separate slices and air-dry for 1–2 hours)
1 qt. vegetable oil (or enough to cover bottom of pan to 1 inch)

Mix all ingredients except bread and oil, and stir in one direction for at least 3 minutes. Trim crusts from bread. Quarter each slice. Spread shrimp mixture evenly over each square. Let stand for 10 minutes.

Heat oil to 400°. Deep-fry, shrimp side down first, until golden brown. Turn once. Drain on paper towel. Serve hot.

SOUR AND SPICY CABBAGE

Serves 8–10 as appetizer

Prepare this cabbage ahead of time, and serve it cold. It tastes best 2–3 days old.

4 T. vegetable oil
2 scallions, cut into 1½-inch strips
2 slices ginger root, cut into very thin strips
3 cloves garlic, minced
4 hot red peppers, cut into strips, or 2 t. minced hot red peppers
6–7 brown peppercorns or 1 t. black pepper

1¼ lb. cabbage, cut into ¼-by-2-inch strips
1½ t. salt
3 T. sugar
3 T. cider vinegar
1 t. sesame oil (optional)

Heat deep pot to high temperature, add vegetable oil, and heat a few seconds. Brown scallions, ginger, and garlic. Add hot peppers and peppercorns or black pepper. Cook a few seconds more.

Stir in cabbage. Stir-fry for about 2 minutes. (Cabbage should be only half-cooked.) Stir in salt, sugar, and vinegar.

Mix well. Remove from heat. Stir in sesame oil if you wish. Cool and refrigerate.

STEAMED PEARL BALLS

Serves 6–8 as appetizer

½ c. sweet rice or short-grain rice
¾ lb. ground pork
2 scallions, chopped
1 t. minced ginger root or ½ t. ginger powder

⅓ c. chopped water chestnuts
¾ t. salt
1 large egg
2 t. cornstarch
1 T. dry white wine

Soak rice in 1½ c. lukewarm water for 2 hours, or in cold water overnight. Drain.

Combine remaining ingredients and 3 T. water. Mix by stirring in one direction until sticky.

Divide pork mixture roughly into 20 parts, roll each piece between palms of hands into a meatball, then roll each meatball in soaked rice.

Place meatballs on aluminum or foil tray. Steam over boiling water for 15 minutes (see p. 5). Serve warm.

STUFFED MUSHROOMS

Serves 8 as appetizer

24 dry mushrooms (1 inch diameter) or fresh mushrooms (1½ inch diameter)
½ c. ground pork
¼ c. chopped cleaned shrimp
1 scallion, chopped
cornstarch

1 T. dry white wine
salt
½ t. minced ginger root or ¼ t. ginger powder
3 lettuce leaves
½ c. chicken broth

If using dry mushrooms, soften them in warm water. Remove mushroom stems carefully so as not to break caps.

Mix pork, shrimp, scallion, 1 T. cornstarch, wine, ⅓ t. salt, and ginger until sticky. Fill each mushroom with stuffing.

Arrange stuffed mushrooms in heatproof tray and steam over boiling water 15 minutes (see p. 5).

Line serving dish with lettuce leaves. Arrange mushrooms on top.

Mix broth and 1½ t. cornstarch, and heat to a boil. Stir and cook 1 minute, or until gravy thickens. Add salt to taste, and pour over stuffed mushrooms.

SUI-MAI DUMPLINGS

Serves 6–8 as appetizer

Serve these dumplings with soy sauce or other favored sauce in a small dish for dipping.

½ c. chopped cleaned shrimp
½ c. ground pork
¼ c. chopped water chestnuts
2 scallions, chopped
1 t. minced ginger root or ½ t.
   ginger powder
1 T. soy sauce

⅓ t. salt
1 egg white
1 T. dry white wine
1 t. cornstarch
1 t. sesame oil
20 wonton skins (see p. 109)

Stir and mix all ingredients (except wonton skins) really well together.

Divide stuffing among wonton skins, placing a portion in center of each. Gather skins up around filling, leaving the skin slightly open and the edges fluted.

Arrange dumplings slightly apart in dish or aluminum pan, set over hot water, and steam at high temperature (see p. 5) for 15 minutes.

CUCUMBER RELISH

Serves 8 as appetizer

2–3 large, slim, firm cucumbers,
   partially pared, cut into halves
   lengthwise, seeds removed
1 t. salt
2 T. sugar

2 T. apple cider vinegar
2 T. vegetable oil
3 garlic cloves, crushed
2 t. minced hot red pepper
few drops sesame oil

Cut each cucumber half lengthwise into 2–3 pieces, then cut crosswise into ½-inch lengths to make ½-inch squares.

Mix cucumber with salt, let stand 1 hour, and drain well. Place in a bowl and stir in sugar and vinegar. Set aside.

Heat small saucepan to medium-high temperature. Add vegetable oil. Heat until very hot. Brown garlic until it turns golden brown. Remove pot from heat. Stir in red pepper and sesame oil.

Slowly pour hot oil mixture over cucumber pieces. Cool to room temperature. Refrigerate at least 1 hour before serving or, even better, refrigerate overnight.

SWEET AND SOUR SHRIMP

Serves 8 as appetizer

To serve this cold as an appetizer, or to go with cocktails, prepare shrimp ahead of time.

1 lb. medium-size raw shrimp in shells	⅓ t. minced hot red pepper
5 scallions	2 T. strawberry-flavored gelatin mix
¼ c. vegetable oil	1 T. sugar
1 t. minced ginger root or ½ t. ginger powder	1 T. cider vinegar
1 t. salt	1½ T. ketchup

Slit back of shrimp about ¼ inch deep, cutting three-fourths of length from head to tail. Devein, rinse, and drain well.

Heat deep pot to high temperature. Cut scallions 2 inches from root end, then cut crosswise in halves (save green tops for other use). Add oil to pot. Heat smoking hot. Add shrimp. Stir-fry until half turns color (about 1 minute).

Add scallions, ginger, salt, and red pepper. Cook another few seconds. Stir in gelatin mix, sugar, vinegar, and ketchup. Stir and cook until shrimp curl up (about ½ minute).

Refrigerate shrimp mixture in covered container for at least 2 hours or overnight.

MAIN DISHES

Beef

BARBECUE—CHINESE FLAVORED

Serves 6–8

3½–4 lbs. boneless sirloin or
    chuck steak, cut into 6–8
    pieces about 1 inch thick
½ c. soy sauce
1½ c. water
½ c. dry white wine

¼ c. brown or white sugar
1 T. sesame or vegetable oil
1 t. white pepper
3–4 garlic cloves, minced
1 t. minced ginger root or ½ t.
    ginger powder

Pound beef with side of heavy knife, or rolling pin, to loosen texture.

Combine remaining ingredients, and marinate beef at least 4 hours, or overnight in refrigerator.

Barbecue on outdoor grill, brushing marinade over meat once or twice while cooking, or cook chuck under oven broiler: Heat broiler tray while preheating the oven, arrange steak pieces in hot tray ½ inch apart. Broil 6 inches under heat for 8 minutes on one side; turn and broil other side another 8–9 minutes. Turn off heat.

For rare meat, take steak out right away; for medium, keep steak in hot oven for 3 minutes; for well done, keep steak in hot oven 8–10 minutes.

BEEF AND BEAN SPROUTS—SPRING ROLL STUFFING #1

Makes 8–12 rolls

¾ lb. flank steak or other lean cut, trimmed
2 T. soy sauce
2 T. dry white wine
2 t. cornstarch
¼ c. vegetable oil
2 scallions, cut into 1½-inch-long strips

1 t. minced ginger root or ½ t. ginger powder
1 small carrot, cut into 1½-inch strips
2 tender celery stalks, cut into 1½-inch strips
1 c. fresh bean sprouts or ½ c. canned bean sprouts, rinsed and drained well
½ t. salt
8 double-layer pancakes (see p. 106) or 12 spring roll skins (see p. 108)

Fillet steak into three thin layers. Cut lengthwise (three layers together) into halves; then cut crosswise into strips.

Marinate beef for 15–30 minutes in soy sauce, wine, and cornstarch. (Add a couple teaspoons of water if beef is hard to stir.)

Heat deep pot to high temperature. Add oil and heat until smoking hot. Stir in beef and quick-fry until three-fourths of beef has changed color. Remove pot from heat. Stir beef until all changes color. Scoop up beef. Set aside.

Return pot to heat. Brown scallions and ginger root a few seconds. Stir in carrot and celery. Quick-fry about ½ minute. Add bean sprouts and salt. Turn off heat. Return beef to pot and gently mix meat with vegetables.

Open pancakes or spring roll skins two-thirds of way. Place stuffing in the middle of each. Roll up to enclose stuffing. Fold one end to prevent juice from leaking while biting from the other end.

BEEF STEAK AND SPINACH

Serves 4–6

1 lb. flank steak or other lean beef
3 T. soy sauce
2 T. cornstarch
½ t. sugar
½ t. baking soda

1 t. onion powder
3 T. vegetable oil
10-oz. pkg. frozen leaf spinach
½ t. salt
3 c. vegetable oil

Trim fat and gristle from beef, and cut meat into 1½-inch cubes.

Combine soy sauce, cornstarch, sugar, soda, and onion powder with ½ c. water. It is important you mix well for at least 2 minutes. Add 3 T. oil. Again mix really well and let stand at least 3 hours (or overnight in the refrigerator).

Place spinach in saucepan. Add salt and ¼ c. water. Cover and cook over medium heat for 13–15 minutes, or until spinach leaves are heated but still green. Spread spinach over bottom of serving dish.

Place 4-qt. pot over medium-high heat, add 3 c. oil, and heat until a cube of bread browns immediately.

Drain beef (save marinade), and add it to hot oil. Brown 1½ minutes; turn each cube over to brown another 1½ minutes. With perforated spoon, remove beef from oil and spread it over spinach.

Bring reserved marinade to a boil. Pour over beef.

GINGER-FLAVORED BEEF SUPREME

Serves 6–8

There are two ways to serve this beef:

In cool weather, cook a 12-oz. package of frozen broccoli or asparagus with ½ t. salt and ¼ c. water just until bright green and crunchy (about 5 minutes over medium-high temperature). Drain. Place cooked beef, juice and all, in the middle of serving dish, and arrange vegetables around it.

In warm weather, cool beef to room temperature and serve it over fresh lettuce.

¼ c. vegetable oil

4–5 thin slices ginger root or 2 t. ginger powder

1½ lb. boneless beef shank or chuck, cut into pieces about ⅓ inch thick, 1 inch long, and ½ inch wide

2 T. dry white wine

¼ c. soy sauce

1½ T. sugar

Heat medium-size pot to high temperature, add oil, and heat for a few seconds. Add ginger, and brown for a few seconds. Stir in beef. Cook until it changes color (about 2 minutes).

Add wine, soy sauce, sugar, and ¼ c. water. Cover. Bring to a rolling boil. Lower heat to medium and simmer (stirring once every 7–8 minutes) 25–30 minutes, or until ¼ c. of juice is left.

BEEF AND BROCCOLI

Serves 4–6

The average Chinese housewife makes quick-fried dishes at least four times a week. Vegetables and meat can be prepared ahead. The cooking takes but a few minutes. Serve this dish with hot rice.

¾ lb. flank steak or other lean beef cut, trimmed

2 T. soy sauce

2 T. dry white wine

2 t. cornstarch

1 t. salt

⅓ c. sliced bamboo shoots

1 small carrot, cut into ¼-inch-thick slices

1 large broccoli, stems peeled, cut lengthwise into 6–8 parts, then cut into about 1-inch lengths (flower and all)

3–4 dry mushrooms, softened in warm water, stems removed, caps cut into thin slices

¼ c. vegetable oil

3 scallions, cut into 1-inch pieces

1 t. minced ginger root or ½ t. ginger powder

1 T. cornstarch and ¼ t. salt, dissolved in ¼ c. water

Split meat lengthwise, then cut crosswise into ¼-inch-thick pieces.

Combine soy sauce, wine, and 2 t. cornstarch, and marinate meat for ½ hour.

Dissolve salt in 2 c. water, add bamboo shoots and carrot, and bring to a boil. Stir in broccoli and mushrooms. Drain as soon as broccoli changes color (about 5 seconds). Set aside.

Heat deep pot to high temperature. Add oil and heat until smoking hot. Stir beef into pot and quick-fry until three-fourths of beef changes color (about 1 minute). Remove pot from heat. Stir until all beef has changed color. Scoop out beef and set aside.

Return pot to heat. Brown scallions and ginger for 15 seconds or so. Add vegetables. Stir in cornstarch mixture and cook until sauce thickens (about 1 minute). Pour vegetables into serving dish. Top with beef.

BEEF AND CABBAGE

Serves 4

¾ lb. flank steak (or other lean beef cut), trimmed
3 T. soy sauce
2 T. dry white wine
1½ t. cornstarch
¼ c. vegetable oil
2 scallions, cut into 1-inch lengths
1 t. minced ginger root or ½ t. ginger powder
2 cloves garlic, chopped
¾ lb. cabbage

Split meat lengthwise into halves, then cut it against the grain into ¼-inch-thick pieces.

Combine 2 T. soy sauce, wine, and cornstarch, and marinate meat ½ hour.

Heat deep pot to high temperature. Add oil. Heat until smoking hot. Quick-fry beef until three-fourths of meat changes color (about 1 minute). Remove pot from heat and stir beef until all changes color. Scoop out beef and set aside.

Return pot to heat. Brown scallions, ginger, and garlic for a few seconds.

Break cabbage into pieces about the size of the beef. Add cabbage, 1 T. soy sauce, and 2 T. water to cooking pot. Lower heat to medium high. Cover and cook 2 minutes, or until cabbage is heated through. Pour into serving dish, juice and all, and top with beef.

FLANK STEAK AND GREEN PEPPERS

Serves 4

¾ lb. flank steak, trimmed
soy sauce
2 T. dry white wine
1 T. cornstarch
½ T. oyster-flavored sauce or ½ t.
    sugar mixed with ½ T. soy
    sauce
¼ c. vegetable oil

2–3 scallions, cut into
    1-inch lengths
2 thin slices ginger root, minced,
    or 1 t. ginger powder
1 t. minced hot red pepper
    (optional)
1 large green pepper
2 medium-size kosher dill pickles,
    sliced

Cut steak lengthwise in half, then slice it crosswise into ⅛-inch pieces. Combine 2 T. soy sauce, wine, cornstarch, and oyster-flavored sauce (or substitute), and marinate beef for ½–1 hour.

Heat deep pot to high temperature. Add oil. Swirl and heat for a few seconds. Stir and fry beef until three-fourths of meat changes color (about 1 minute). Remove pot from heat. Stir until all beef changes color (8–10 seconds). Scoop out and set aside.

Return pot to heat. Brown scallions, ginger, and red pepper (if you wish to use it) for a few seconds.

Cut green pepper into pieces about the size of the beef, and add to pot. Add pickles, and stir-fry 10–12 seconds. Stir in 1 t. soy sauce. Spread mixture on bottom of serving dish and top with the cooked beef.

ROAST CHUCK—CHINESE FLAVORED

Serves 8–12

4-pound bone-in chuck or rib roast
⅓ c. soy sauce
2 T. dry white wine
2 scallions, cut into 1-inch lengths

½ T. sugar
1 whole anise, separated, or 1 t. five-fragrance spice powder

Marinate roast in remaining ingredients for 3 hours or, for best results, overnight in refrigerator.

Put roast, marinade juice, and 1½ c. water in porcelain enamel roaster. Cover and roast in 300° oven for about 2 hours.

This meat tastes delicious served hot or cold.

SHISH KEBAB—CHINESE FLAVORED

Serves 8–10

You can serve these shish kebabs in various ways: Serve off the stick, as regular shish kebab. Or wrap barbecued beef and vegetables in double-layer pancakes (see p. 106) and eat with hands. Or brush shish kebabs with hot sauce mixture of ¼ c. soy sauce, 1½ T. sugar, 2 t. garlic powder, and 1 t. minced hot red pepper.

2–2¼ lb. flank steak or other favored tender cut, trimmed
¼ c. soy sauce
¼ c. dry white wine
3 scallions, cut into ½-inch lengths
2 slices ginger root, minced, or 1 t. ginger powder

1 t. sugar
1 t. sesame oil
2 T. vegetable oil
½ t. black pepper
2 large green peppers, cut into about 40 pieces
1 large onion, cut and separated into about 40 disk-shaped pieces

Cut meat lengthwise in half, then slice it against the grain ¼ inch thick to make 60 pieces.

Combine soy sauce, wine, scallions, ginger, sugar, oils, and black pepper, and marinate beef for 2 hours, or overnight in refrigerator.

Using 20 small shish kebab sticks, thread a piece of green pepper; lace through a piece of beef; top with a piece of onion followed by a piece of beef. Continue until there are 3 pieces of beef, 2 pieces of green pepper, and 2 pieces of onion on each stick.

Barbecue over medium-high charcoal flame for about 1 minute; turn once.

STEWED CHUCK STEAK WITH POTATOES

Serves 4–6

1½ lb. first-cut bone-in chuck steak
3 T. vegetable oil
2 scallions, cut into 1-inch pieces
2 thin slices ginger root or ½ t. ginger powder

2 T. dry white wine
2½ T. soy sauce
1 t. brown or white sugar
2–3 potatoes (about ¾ lb.)
2 c. vegetable oil

Remove bone and part of fat from steak, and cut meat into 1-inch cubes.

Heat medium-size deep pot to high temperature. Add 3 T. oil, heat for a few seconds, and brown scallions and ginger. Add beef. Stir and cook until meat changes color. Add wine, soy sauce, and 2½ c. water. Bring to a rolling boil. Cover and cook over medium-high temperature for ½ hour.

Lower heat to medium. Stir in sugar. Simmer 15 minutes longer (or until beef is tender). Stir occasionally while cooking.

While beef is cooking, peel potatoes, cut them into triangles about the same size as beef, rinse, and drain well. Heat another pot to medium-high temperature. Add 2 c. oil. Heat until very hot (about 1 minute). Deep-fry potatoes until golden brown on the outside and cooked in the center. Drain on paper towels.

Spread potatoes on bottom of serving dish. Top with cooked beef, juice and all.

TWICE-COOKED BEEF SHANK

Serves 4–6

Serve this beef and its juices over hot spaghetti or rice.

2¼–2½ lbs. bone-in beef shank
2 scallions, cut in half
1 thick slice ginger root, chopped, or 1 t. ginger powder
3 T. vegetable oil

1 large leek, cut into 1½-inch lengths
½ t. minced hot red pepper
3 T. soy sauce
1 t. sugar

Remove bones from beef shank, and cut meat into about 1½-inch cubes.

In pressure cooker, bring 1½ qt. water to a boil. Add beef, scallions, and ginger, and cook under 10 lb. pressure for 25 minutes. (If regular pot is used, simmer beef with scallions and ginger for 2–2½ hours, or until beef is tender.) Cool pressure cooker 10 minutes. Rinse under cold water and release pressure. Scoop up beef and drain (save beef broth for other use).

Heat deep pot to high temperature. Add oil. Heat for a few seconds. Quick-fry leek for about ½ minute. Add red pepper and beef. Stir. Cover and cook for about 1 minute. Stir in soy sauce and sugar. Mix well.

TWICE-COOKED BEEF TRIPE

Serves 4

½ lb. beef tripe
salt
¼ lb. lean pork, cut into 1-inch
   strips
2 T. dry white wine
1 t. cornstarch
¼ c. vegetable oil
3 garlic cloves, crushed

3 scallions, cut into 1-inch strips
1 t. minced ginger root or ½ t.
   ginger powder
1 t. minced hot red pepper
   (optional)
2 celery stalks, cut lengthwise into
   1-inch strips

Rub tripe with 1 t. salt, squeeze and rub for 2 minutes, rinse well, and drain.

Bring 1 qt. water to a boil. Put in beef tripe. Cover and simmer ½ hour (or until tender). Drain. Cut into 1-inch strips.

Marinate pork for 15 minutes in wine, ¼ t. salt, and cornstarch.

Heat deep pot to high temperature. Add oil. Quick-fry pork until meat changes color (about 1 minute). Scoop up and set aside.

Brown garlic, scallion, ginger, and red pepper (if you like) for a few minutes. Stir in celery. Cook ½ minute. Add ⅓ t. salt. Stir in tripe and pork. Stir gently just until blended.

Complete Meals

CHINESE DUMPLINGS—BOILED, FRIED, OR STEAMED ("THE FAMILY AFFAIR")

Serves 4–6

The cook of the family prepares the stuffing and dough ahead of time. The rest of the family helps in rolling the skins and making dumplings. It is a time-consuming job (about two hours of constant work), but it sure makes a restless rainy Sunday afternoon cozy and memorable. (Chinese college students here and abroad turn "Dumpling Making" into "Match Making.") Dumplings can be served plain or with soy sauce.

To avoid problems, keep the following helpful hints in mind:

Refrigerate dumplings if not cooked immediately after being made.

Ready-made dumplings can be frozen individually. Boil when still frozen. It will take longer for the second boil.

Do not pile up cooked dumplings.

BOILED DUMPLINGS

2 c. flour   stuffing: see p. 51 for combination
¾ c. water   you like

Add water, a few drops at a time, to flour until well blended. Knead and squeeze into a ball. Let stand, covered with wet paper towel, at room temperature for ½ hour.

Mix stuffing ingredients, stirring in one direction, until sticky. (Add a couple tablespoons of water if stuffing appears to be hard to stir.) Set aside.

Knead dough thoroughly on floured board until smooth (allow at least 10 minutes of hard kneading). Divide dough into 32 pieces. Roll each piece into a ball, then flatten into the size of a silver dollar. With rolling pin, roll each piece of dough into a round skin about 1½ inches in diameter.

Hold a skin in one hand. Place 1 T. stuffing in center of skin. Fold skin in half across the filling and pinch open edges together to seal in filling.

Fill deep pot two-thirds full of water. Bring water to a rolling boil. Drop dumplings in, one by one. Gently stir with chopsticks or wooden spoon to separate dumplings. Bring to a second boil. Add ½ c. cold water. Stir and bring to a third boil. Add another ½ c. cold water. Bring to a final boil. Scoop dumplings out with perforated spoon.

FRIED DUMPLINGS

2 c. flour
¾ c. + 1 T. boiling water

stuffing: see p. 51 and choose one
    combination
¼ c. vegetable oil

Stir boiling water, a few drops at a time, into flour until well blended. Knead and squeeze mixture into a ball. Cover with wet paper towel and let stand at room temperature for ½ hour.

Mix stuffing, knead dough, and make dumplings in the same manner as for boiled dumplings (see preceding recipe).

Heat electric frying pan or skillet to 350°. Add oil. Swirl pan to coat bottom evenly. Heat oil for 1 minute. Place dumplings slightly apart. Fry until bottom of dumplings turns golden brown. Add ½ c. cold water. Cover and cook until water evaporates (in about 10 minutes). Check closely during last few minutes of cooking. (If regular frying pan is used, fry 16 dumplings at a time over medium-high temperature. Cut oil, water, and cooking time in half.)

Scoop up dumplings and place each in serving dish with browned side up so it stays crunchy.

STEAMED DUMPLINGS

2 c. flour
¾ c. + 1 T. boiling water

stuffing: choose one combination
    from p. 51

Prepare dough the same way as for fried dumplings (see preceding recipe).

Mix stuffing, knead dough, and make dumplings the same way as boiled dumplings (see p. 49).

Line steamer with 2-by-2-inch wax paper squares—as many as can fit in without overlapping. Place a dumpling on each square. Steam over boiling water for 12 minutes.

STUFFINGS FOR CHINESE DUMPLINGS

SHRIMP STUFFING

6 oz. cleaned shrimp, chopped
6 oz. ground pork
2 scallions, chopped
7–8 water chestnuts, chopped
1 t. minced ginger root or ½ t.
   ginger powder

¾ t. salt
1 large egg
2 t. cornstarch
few drops sesame oil (optional)

PORK STUFFING

12 oz. finely chopped or ground
   pork
3 scallions, chopped
1 t. minced ginger root or ½ t.
   ginger powder
1½ c. chopped Chinese cabbage
   or cabbage heart, mixed with
   ½ t. salt, allowed to stand 15
   minutes, then squeezed

1 large egg
1 T. cornstarch
⅔ t. salt
2 T. dry white wine
1 t. sesame oil
¼ c. chicken broth

BEEF STUFFING

12 oz. ground round or sirloin
½ c. chopped onion
3–4 dry mushrooms, softened in
   water, stems removed, caps
   chopped, or ½ c. chopped
   fresh mushrooms

1 t. minced ginger root or ½ t.
   ginger powder
1 large egg
1 T. cornstarch
2 T. dry white wine
½ c. chicken broth

FISH STUFFING

1 lb. fresh, firm fillet of flounder
   or other white fish fillet,
   chopped
3 scallions, chopped
1½ t. minced ginger root or ½ t.
   ginger powder

2 T. dry white wine
1 large egg
1 T. cornstarch
1 t. salt

VEGETARIAN'S FAVORITE

Combine the following and cook as scrambled eggs, using 2 T. vegetable oil:

6 large eggs
½ t. salt

½ t. black pepper
2 T. water

Cool to room temperature. Chop. Then add the following:

½ c. chopped fresh mushrooms
½ c. squeezed defrosted frozen
   chopped spinach
2 scallions, chopped

2 T. cornstarch
⅓ t. salt
1 t. sesame oil

HOT POT COOKERY

This is one of the easiest and coziest ways to enjoy a relaxed dinner with close friends in cold weather.

The best thing about hot pot cookery is that the cook of the family doesn't have to do any cooking at the time of entertaining. All she, or he, has to do is to gather all the ingredients, clean and cut them into desired sizes and shapes, arrange them attractively on several large platters, then set up broth in either a Chinese hot pot or an electric skillet in the middle of the dining table. With fondue forks and chopsticks, each person cooks and seasons his own food, as one does with fondue. A bottle of wine adds to the festivities.

To plan the menu, allow the following amount per person with an average appetite: ¾ lb. meat, poultry, and seafood; ¼ lb. vegetables; ¼ lb. starch.

The following is an example, with ingredients listed in suggested serving order, to serve 4:

2 qt. chicken broth. Fill hot pot, or skillet, to 1½ inches below the rim. Keep extra broth hot in pot on the stove for refill.

4–5 scallions. Cut into 1½-inch lengths.

2 thin slices ginger root or 1 t. ginger powder.

½ c. bamboo shoot slices.

4–5 dry mushrooms. Soften in warm water, discard stems, quarter caps.

1 lb. medium shrimp in shells. Slit back of shrimp about ¼ inch deep, cutting three-fourths of length from head to tail. Devein, rinse, and drain well.

1 lb. fillet of flounder, or other white firm fish fillet. Cut into 1-inch squares.

¾ lb. boneless, skinless chicken breast. Remove cartilage. Cut into ¼-inch-thick slices.

¾ lb. flank steak, or other lean beef. Cut lengthwise in halves, then cut crosswise into ¼-inch slices.

6 oz. fresh spinach. Rinse and drain.

6–8 Chinese cabbage leaves (yellow, tender inside leaves only). Cut crosswise, stems and all, into 1-inch lengths.

1 small bundle cellophane noodles. Soften in hot water and drain. Or ¼ lb. thin spaghetti. Cook, rinse in cold water, and drain.

SAUCES

Choose at least two kinds to go with hot pot cooking.

2 T. vegetable oil

3 cloves garlic, minced

1 t. minced hot red pepper

¼ c. soy sauce

1½ T. sugar

Heat small saucepan to medium-high temperature. Add oil. Brown garlic until it turns brown and smells good. Add pepper. Stir in soy sauce and sugar. Bring to a boil. Serve hot or cold.

½ c. cider vinegar
1½ t. minced ginger root

Mix and serve.

¼ c. soy sauce   1 t. minced hot red pepper
¼ c. cider vinegar   few drops sesame oil

Mix well and serve.

½ c. soy sauce
¼ t. sesame oil

Mix.

½ c. ketchup   2 t. garlic powder
2 T. grated horseradish   2 t. black pepper

Combine and mix well.

¼ c. cider vinegar   2 T. sherry
¼ c. sugar   1 T. cornstarch, dissolved in
1½ T. ketchup   ¼ c. water
1 T. soy sauce

Mix all ingredients except cornstarch mixture in small saucepan. Heat to a boil, then stir in cornstarch mixture. Cook until sauce thickens (about 30 seconds).

Fish

BOILED FRESH FLOUNDER

Serves 4–6

1 T. salt
2–2¼ lbs. fresh flounder, cleaned
    but head left on
3 scallions, cut into 1½-inch strips
2 t. minced ginger root or 1 t.
    ginger powder
1 t. white pepper
2 T. vegetable oil

3 slices bacon, cut into 1-inch
    lengths
3 T. soy sauce
4 T. cider vinegar
4 T. sugar
2 T. cornstarch, dissolved in ¼ c.
    water

In a covered pan big enough to accommodate fish, bring 2 qt. water and salt to a boil. Place fish in water. Cover and bring to another boil. Lower heat to medium and slow-boil fish for 3 minutes. Turn off heat, but keep fish covered for 10 more minutes.

Reserving cooking liquid, remove fish and place it on heated platter. Sprinkle scallions, ginger, and pepper over fish.

In small saucepan, heat oil to medium-high temperature. Brown bacon until crisp.

Meanwhile, quickly measure out 2½ c. stock from the fish cooking liquid. Add to it the remaining ingredients, then stir mixture into bacon pan. Stir and cook until sauce thickens (about 2 minutes). Gently pour over fish and serve immec..ately.

FISH FILLET WITH MEAT SAUCE

Serves 4 –6

1 lb. fillet of flounder or other firm white fish fillet
2 c. vegetable oil (or enough to cover bottom of pan ½ inch)
½ c. cornstarch
2 cloves garlic, chopped
½ c. ground pork
1 t. minced hot red pepper (optional)

1 T. dry white wine
1 T. soy sauce
1 T. cornstarch, dissolved in 1 c. water
1 T. sugar
1 T. wine vinegar
1 t. salt

Rinse fish, dry between paper towels, and cut into ½-by-1-inch pieces.

Heat deep pot to high temperature. Add oil. Turn heat to medium-high. Heat oil until cube of white bread browns immediately.

Coat fish pieces, one by one, with cornstarch. Drop each into pot, and brown both sides until golden brown (2–3 minutes on each side). Drain on paper towel. Put in serving dish and keep hot.

Remove all but 2 T. oil from pot. Brown garlic. Add pork and stir and cook until pork changes color.

Add red pepper if you wish, then quickly mix remaining ingredients and stir them in. Bring sauce to a boil, lower heat, and stir until sauce thickens (about 3 minutes).

Pour sauce over fish and serve hot.

GOLDEN BROWN FISH FILLET WITH BACON

Serves 4

2 qt. vegetable oil (or enough to
    cover bottom of pan to 1½
    inches)
2 large eggs
2 egg yolks
¾ c. flour
1 t. salt

1 t. onion powder
4 medium-size slices fillet of
    flounder (about 1¼ lbs.)
4 leaves romaine lettuce
4 slices bacon
black pepper (optional)

Heat oil in electric frying pan to 400°.

Combine eggs, egg yolks, flour, salt, and onion powder, and beat with electric mixer for 3 minutes. Batter should be similar to pancake batter.

Rinse flounder and dry well with paper towels. Rinse lettuce, dry with paper towels, and cut to the same size as the fish. Trim off part of the hard end of the stem.

Make a sandwich with slice of fish fillet in the middle, a slice of bacon on one side, a leaf of lettuce on the other. Dip "sandwich" into batter until well coated. Deep-fry until golden brown (about 7 minutes on each side).

Cut each sandwich into three. Serve hot with a sprinkle of black pepper, if preferred.

OVEN-STEWED CARP

Serves 8–12

4–4½ lbs. whole fresh carp
1 t. salt
¼ c. vegetable oil
3 t. minced ginger root or 1 t. ginger powder
¼ c. chopped bamboo shoots
3–4 dry mushrooms, softened in warm water, stems discarded, caps chopped, or ⅓ lb. fresh mushrooms, stems and caps chopped

1 small carrot, chopped
½ t. minced hot red pepper (optional)
3 T. soy sauce
2 T. cornstarch
2 T. dry white wine
4 scallions, chopped

Make 5 slashes on each side of carp. Cut crosswise, making 2 sections. Dry with paper towels. Rub fish inside and out with salt.

Heat deep pot to medium-high temperature, add oil, and heat until smoking hot. Brown fish, one section at a time, until brown crust is formed on skin. Turn once. Remove fish from pot and place in shallow covered ovenproof dish.

In leftover oil in pot, brown ginger for about 8 seconds. Stir in bamboo shoots, mushrooms, carrot, and red pepper if you wish. Cook ½ minute.

Combine soy sauce, cornstarch, and wine with 1½ c. water, and stir into pot. Pour over fish. Cover.

Bake in 350° oven for 1¼–1½ hours, spooning sauce over fish occasionally. Sprinkle scallions over fish before serving.

PEPPERCORN-FLAVORED FRESH FISH

Serves 4

For this recipe, the fresher the fish, the better the taste—don't try to substitute frozen and defrosted fish.

2 whole fresh 1-lb. silver bass, or other fish, cleaned	1½ t. salt
1½ t. brown peppercorns or 1 t. black pepper	¼ c. vegetable oil

Remove fish heads if you wish, and make two ¼-inch slashes on each side of fish. Rinse and dry with paper towel, inside and out. Rub fish with pepper and salt, inside and out. Let stand for ½ hour at room temperature.

Heat frying pan to high temperature (400°). Add oil. Heat until very hot. Brown fish until skin hardens (do not move fish until skin turns golden brown; otherwise it sticks to bottom of pan). Turn and brown second side. To judge if fish is thoroughly cooked, examine the slash. When there is no trace of blood left on the bone, the fish is done.

QUICK-STEWED FISH STEAKS

Serves 4

1¼–1½ lb. 1-inch-thick fish steaks	1 t. minced hot red pepper (optional)
3 T. vegetable oil	
3 scallions, cut into 1½-inch lengths	2 T. dry white wine
	3 T. soy sauce
1 garlic clove, crushed	1 t. sugar

Rinse fish and dry it between paper towels. Heat frying pan to high temperature. Add oil. Heat until smoking hot. Brown fish 6–8 minutes on one side. Turn and brown other side 5–6 minutes. Remove fish from pan and set aside.

Brown scallions and garlic until they smell good (about ½ minute). Add red pepper if you wish, and return fish to pan. Pour wine over fish. Add soy sauce, sugar, and ⅔ c. water. Cover and bring to a boil.

Lower heat and simmer until sauce thickens to ½ cup (about 8 minutes). Shove fish around a little and spoon sauce over a few times while stewing.

QUICK-STEWED WHOLE FISH

Serves 4–6

2¼–2½ lbs. whole red snapper, porgy, or striped bass, cleaned but head left on
⅔ t. salt
⅔ c. vegetable oil
4 scallions, cut into 1½-inch strips
2 t. minced ginger root or 1 t. ginger powder
¼ c. shredded bamboo shoots or celery
¼ c. shredded carrots
2 T. soy sauce
1½ T. cornstarch
2 T. dry white wine

Remove fish gills. Rinse and dry fish with paper towels. Make 3 slanted slashes on each side. Rub fish, inside and out, with salt. Let stand 10 minutes.

Heat electric frying pan to 400° (high temperature on stove setting). Add oil. Heat oil until smoking hot. Brown fish on one side until brown crust forms on skin (about 8 minutes). Turn and brown reverse side. Remove fish and set aside.

Brown scallions and ginger for about 10 seconds. Stir in bamboo shoots or celery and carrots. Quickly fry for a few seconds.

Combine remaining ingredients with 1½ c. water. Stir mixture into pan and bring to rolling boil.

Return fish to pan. Cover and simmer at 300–325° about 25 minutes, shoving fish around a little and spooning gravy over it occasionally.

Place fish in warm serving platter, and pour gravy over it.

SMOKE-FLAVORED FISH STEAKS

Serves 8–12

Prepare these steaks ahead of time and serve them cold as part of a platter or by themselves as appetizer. Use any big-boned firm fresh fish.

2½–3 lb. 1-inch-thick fish steaks
¼ c. soy sauce
¼ c. cider vinegar
¼ c. sugar
½ t. hickory-smoke salt
2 t. five-fragrance spice powder
4 scallions, cut into ½-inch
   lengths

2 t. minced ginger root or 1 t.
   ginger powder
¼ c. dry white wine
1 qt. vegetable oil (or enough to
   cover bottom of pan to 1½
   inches)

Marinate fish steaks overnight in refrigerator in a mixture of all the remaining ingredients except oil. Turn occasionally.

Drain fish and air-dry 3–4 hours. Save marinade.

Heat deep pot to high temperature. Add oil. Heat until cube of white bread browns immediately. Reduce heat to medium high.

Deep-fry fish (don't crowd pieces—do one batch at a time) until edges turn dark brown (4–5 minutes). Turn fish over and fry another 4–5 minutes. Save oil, and drain fish on paper towels.

Again soak deep-fried fish steaks in marinade for 3 hours, or overnight in refrigerator. Drain and air-dry 2–3 hours.

Deep-fry in medium-high oil for another 3 minutes on each side. Drain on paper towels. Chill completely before serving.

STEAMED FLOUNDER

Serves 4

2–2½-lb. whole fresh flounder,
   cleaned but head left on
⅔ t. salt
2 T. vegetable oil
2 garlic cloves, crushed
½ c. ground pork
1 T. cornstarch, dissolved in ¾ c.
   water
2 T. soy sauce

2 T. dry white wine
1 small carrot, cut into thin strips
4–5 scallions, cut into 2-inch
    lengths, then into thin strips
2 thick slices ginger root, cut into
   thin strips, or 1 t. ginger powder
½ t. sesame oil

Make three ½-inch-deep slashes on dark side of fish. Rub salt inside and out of flounder. Place fish in large heatproof dish, dark side up, and steam over 3 inches boiling water for 20 minutes.

Heat medium-size pan to high temperature. Add vegetable oil. Brown garlic 10–15 seconds. Stir in pork. Cook until meat changes color. Stir in cornstarch mix, soy sauce, and wine. Bring to rolling boil. Add carrot strips. Stir and cook until carrot strips turn soft (about 1 minute). Turn off heat.

Sprinkle scallions, ginger, and sesame oil over steamed fish. Pour sauce over all and serve hot.

SWEET AND SOUR FISH FILLET

Serves 4–6

1¼ lb. fillet of flounder or other
   white firm fish fillet
½ t. salt
1 qt. vegetable oil (or enough to
   cover bottom of pan to 1½
   inches)
½ c. cornstarch

2 garlic cloves, crushed
¼ c. sugar
¼ c. apple cider vinegar
1 c. water
1 T. cornstarch
3 T. soy sauce

Cut fish into pieces about 1 by 2 inches, dry between paper towels, mix with salt, and let stand a few minutes.

Heat oil to medium-high temperature (375°) while placing a few pieces of fish into bag with ½ cup cornstarch. Shake bag to coat fish. Continue adding fish pieces until all are coated.

Deep-fry fish until pieces turn light brown, turning once (allow 2–3 minutes on each side). Drain fish on paper towels. Keep oil in pan.

Take 2 T. oil from fryer and place in medium-size pot. Heat to medium-high temperature. Brown garlic until it turns color and smells good. Stir in remaining ingredients. Mix and cook until sauce thickens (about 2 minutes).

Reheat oil in frying pan to high temperature (400°). Return cooked fish to oil. Deep-fry until golden brown (about 1 minute). Drain and place in serving dish. Pour sauce over fish just before serving, so fish stays crispy.

SWEET AND SOUR WHOLE FISH

Serves 4–6

2¼–2½ lbs. whole fresh red snapper or other big-boned saltwater fish, cleaned

1 t. salt

1 t. minced ginger root or 1 t. ginger powder

2 T. dry white wine

2 qt. vegetable oil (or enough to cover bottom of pan to 2 inches)

½ c. flour

¼ c. shredded carrots

3 T. sugar

3 T. apple cider vinegar

2 T. soy sauce

1 T. cornstarch, dissolved in ½ c. water

4 scallions, cut into 2-inch strips

1 T. shredded ginger root

Make 3–4 slashes ½ inch deep on each side of fish. Remove head if you prefer. Combine salt, ginger root or 1 t. ginger powder dissolved in 1 t. water, and wine, and rub fish, inside and out, with mixture. Let stand for ½ hour.

In frying pan large enough to accommodate fish, heat oil to high temperature (400°).

Spread flour on paper towel. Place fish on top. Shake and fold towel to coat fish with flour.

Deep-fry fish until golden brown and cooked (allow at least 7–8 minutes on each side).

While fish is frying, heat medium-size pot to medium-high temperature. Add 2 T. oil from frying pan. Quick-fry carrots about 30 seconds. Stir in sugar, vinegar, soy sauce, and cornstarch mixture. Cook until sauce thickens (about 2 minutes).

Place cooked fish in serving dish. Spread scallions and shredded ginger root over fish. Gently pour sauce over fish. Serve hot.

Pork

EGGPLANT WITH MEAT SAUCE

Serves 6–8 as side dish

¼ c. vegetable oil
3 garlic cloves, crushed
1 T. chopped scallions
½ t. minced ginger root or ½ t. ginger powder
½ c. chopped or ground pork

2 medium-size slim, firm eggplants (1–1¼ lb.), quartered and cut into bite-size triangles
3 T. soy sauce
2 t. sugar
1 c. chicken or pork broth
salt

Heat deep pot to high temperature, add oil, and heat for a few seconds. Fry garlic until golden brown. Stir in scallions, ginger, and pork. Quick-fry until meat changes color.

Add eggplant pieces, mix well, then add remaining ingredients. Mix well, cover, and simmer (stirring occasionally) over medium heat for 15 minutes, or until eggplant is tender.

GOLDEN BROWN STUFFED EGGPLANT

Serves 4 as main dish, 8 as appetizer

2 slim, firm eggplants (about ½ lb.)

½ lb. ground pork

2 T. chopped water chestnuts

1 T. soy sauce

1 t. cornstarch, dissolved with 1 T. water

2 large eggs

½ c. flour

1 t. garlic powder

½ t. salt

2 T. bread crumbs

1 qt. vegetable oil (or enough to cover bottom of pan to 2 inches)

Cut eggplants lengthwise into halves, then cut crosswise into ½-inch-thick half-moon-shaped slices. Slit slices, from skin side, two-thirds of way toward cut side to make a pocket for stuffing.

Mix pork, water chestnuts, soy sauce, and cornstarch mixture, stirring in one direction until sticky. Press 1 rounded teaspoonful of stuffing into each eggplant pocket.

Beat eggs, flour, garlic powder, salt, and bread crumbs until well blended.

Heat oil to medium-high temperature (375°). Dip stuffed eggplant slices, stuffed side down, into batter. Deep-fry until golden brown, turning once. Drain on paper towels.

JELLIED PORK HOCKS

Serves 6–8

Prepare this ahead, and serve it as part of dinner in warm weather.

3–3½ lbs. pork hocks

2 t. salt

1 t. black pepper

½ t. baking soda

3–4 lettuce leaves

radish roses (optional)

Remove hair from hocks with tweezers, rinse, and dry with paper towels. Remove bones from hocks.

Soak hocks in salt, pepper, soda, and 2 c. lukewarm water. Refrigerate overnight.

Put hocks, juice and all, into deep pot. Bring to a boil and simmer 1½ hours, or until ½ cup juice is left. Stir occasionally while cooking. Pour hocks, juice and all, into pound cake baking pan or mold. Refrigerate until gelatin is set (about 3 hours).

Trim off layer of fat from top. Slice hocks into ¼-inch pieces.

To serve, line surface of dish with lettuce. Arrange hock slices on top of lettuce. Top with radish roses if you wish.

MEATBALL DAISY

Serves 8

This dish is not only an attractive centerpiece but a delicious main-meal dish. The meatball can be cooked ahead of time: before serving, reheat meatball and juice in deep pot over medium-high temperature for 10–15 minutes. Make flower-shaped omelet while meatball is being reheated.

1¼ lb. ground pork or meatloaf mix of pork, veal, and beef
2 scallions, chopped
1 t. minced ginger root or ½ t. ginger powder
¼ c. chopped water chestnuts or bamboo shoots
2–3 dry mushroom caps, softened in warm water, then chopped, or ¼ c. chopped fresh mushrooms

4 large eggs
2 T. cornstarch
salt
2 T. dry white wine
1½ c. chicken or pork broth
1 qt. vegetable oil (or enough to cover bottom of pot to 3 inches)
2 T. flour
1 T. vegetable oil

Mix meat, scallions, ginger, water chestnuts or bamboo shoots, mushrooms, 1 egg, cornstarch, 1¼ t. salt, wine, and ½ c. broth, stirring in one direction for 4–5 minutes, or until mixture is sticky. Wet hands. Form meat mixture into a ball. Then gently toss it from one hand to the other until it is free of holes and cracks.

Heat medium-size deep pot to medium-high temperature. Add 1 qt. oil. Heat until cube of fresh bread turns golden brown immediately when dropped into oil. Deep-fry meatball until a light brown crust forms on bottom side (about 3 minutes). Gently turn and fry other side another 2–3 minutes.

Carefully scoop up meatball and place in a heat-resistant bowl. Add 1 c. broth. Steam over boiling water for 1 hour. (Add more boiling water when necessary.)

Combine 3 eggs, flour, ⅓ t. salt, and 1 T. water with electric mixer or by hand until well blended.

Heat a 12-inch fryer to medium-high temperature. Add 1 T. oil. Swirl to cover bottom of pan. Heat for a few seconds. Pour batter into pan. Swirl pan to make an even layer. Lower heat to medium. Cover and cook 1–1½ minutes, or until omelet is set. Cool omelet in pan 2–3 minutes.

Scallop edges of omelet to resemble a daisy, as illustrated.

Line omelet "flower" on bottom of shallow serving dish. Place meatball in center. Pour juice over meatball. Serve hot.

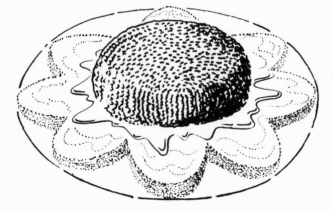

MU-HSU PORK—SPRING ROLL STUFFING #2

Serves 4 as main dish; makes 8 spring rolls

¾ lb. lean pork, cut against the grain into about 1-inch-square thin slices

¼ t. salt

2 T. soy sauce

2 T. dry white wine

2 t. cornstarch

¼ c. vegetable oil

2 scallions, cut into 1-inch lengths

1 t. minced ginger root or ½ t. ginger powder

10–12 fresh spinach leaves, rinsed, drained, broken into halves

½ c. dry wood ears, softened in warm water, drained, or 4–5 dry mushrooms, softened in warm water, stems removed, caps cut into thin slices

3 large eggs, beaten with ⅓ t. salt

8 double-layer pancakes (see p. 106) or 12 spring roll skins (see p. 108)

Marinate pork for ½ hour in salt, 1 T. soy sauce, wine, and cornstarch. If pork appears to be too dry (hard to mix), add a little water, a few drops at a time.

Heat deep pot to high temperature. Add oil. Heat oil until smoking hot. Quick-fry pork until meat changes color (about 2 minutes). Scoop up pork. Set aside.

Brown scallions and ginger for about 10 seconds. Add spinach and mushrooms. Stir fry until spinach just changes color. Stir in egg mix and cook until egg is set (about 1 minute). Turn off heat. Return pork to pot. Stir in 1 T. soy sauce and mix well.

To eat, divide pork among pancakes or skins. Roll up to enclose stuffing. Bite from one end of roll while holding folded other end, to prevent juice from leaking.

OVEN-STEWED LION'S HEAD

Serves 6–8

2 lb. ground pork	2 t. salt
2 scallions, chopped	2 T. vegetable oil
1 t. minced ginger root or ½ t. ginger powder	1 small cabbage (about 1½ lb.), quartered, broken into about 2-inch squares
1 large egg	
2 T. dry white wine	2 c. chicken broth
1 T. cornstarch, dissolved in ¼ c. water	

Place pork, scallions, ginger, egg, wine, cornstarch mixture, and 1½ t. salt in bowl. Stir in one direction until sticky (8–10 minutes). Divide mixture into 6 even portions. With wet hands, form each into a ball. Set aside.

Heat deep pot to high temperature. Add oil. Heat for a few seconds. Stir in cabbage and ½ t. salt. Quick-fry for 1 minute.

Spread two-thirds of cabbage over bottom of porcelain enameled roaster. Place meatballs on cabbage. Cover with remaining cabbage. Pour chicken broth over all. Cover and bake in 300° oven for 1½–1¾ hours.

PORK SHOULDER ROLL

Serves 4–8

Prepare this pork several days ahead of time and serve as cold cuts.

2 lb. pork shoulder (from skinny end)	1 t. brown or black peppercorns
	1½ T. salt

Split pork lengthwise all the way to the bone. Remove bone carefully so meat and skin stay in one whole piece.

In small saucepan, toast peppercorns and salt over medium-high heat until salt turns light brown and smells good (about 5 minutes). Stir and shake pan while toasting.

Rub pepper-salt all over pork. Roll up pork from one cut end (with skin on outside). Run a cord around pork from one end to the other, then a few times horizontally, so the roll won't loosen. Refrigerate 2–3 days.

Place roll in medium-size deep pot. Add water to cover roll completely. Cover pot and bring to a boil. Let simmer for 2 hours.

Drain and chill roll completely. Remove cord. Slice thin.

POT-ROASTED PORK SHOULDER

Serves 4–6

1 T. vegetable oil
2–2¼ lb. pork shoulder, skinny end only
3 scallions, cut into 1-inch lengths
2 thin slices ginger root or 1 t. ginger powder
1 whole anise or 1 t. five-fragrance spice powder

4–5 brown or black peppercorns
¼ c. soy sauce
2 T. dry white wine
2 pieces rock candy (about size of large grape) or 2 T. dark brown sugar

Heat medium-size deep pot to medium-high temperature. Add oil. Swirl to cover bottom of pot. Brown pork shoulder on all sides. Remove pork and set aside.

Brown scallions and ginger for a few seconds. Add anise or spice powder, pepper, soy sauce, wine, and 2 c. boiling water. Return pork to pot. Cover and bring to a rolling boil. Lower heat to medium or low. Simmer for 2½–3 hours (turning occasionally while stewing), or until pork is very tender and the sauce thickens to ⅔ cup.

Add rock candy or brown sugar. Stir until it melts. Simmer another hour.

Discard anise and peppercorns. Remove bone from pork and cut lengthwise into 4–6 portions, skin and all. Serve with sauce.

QUICK-STEWED PORK BUTT AND STRING BEANS

Serves 4–6

This dish tastes very good served over cooked rice or spaghetti.

2 T. vegetable oil

2 scallions, cut into 1-inch lengths

2 garlic cloves, crushed

1¼ lb. fresh boneless pork butt, diced (fat and all)

1 lb. tender string beans, cut into 1-inch lengths

2 T. dry white wine

3 T. soy sauce

½ T. sugar

Heat deep pot to high temperature. Add oil and heat for a few seconds. Brown scallions and garlic. Stir in pork. Quick-fry until meat changes color (about 1 minute). Scoop up meat and set aside.

Stir beans into pot. Stir and cook until beans change into dark green (2–3 minutes). Return pork to pot.

Add wine, soy sauce, sugar, and ¼ c. water. Bring to a boil. Cover and simmer over medium-high heat until beans are tender (about 12 minutes).

SWEET AND SOUR MEATBALLS

Serves 4–6

12 oz. ground pork
1 scallion, chopped
½ t. salt
1 large egg
1 T. cornstarch
1 qt. vegetable oil (or enough to
cover bottom of pot to 1½
inches)
2 cloves garlic, chopped
6 medium-size Italian green
peppers, each cut lengthwise
into 4 pieces

2 rings canned pineapple, each cut
into 8 pieces
2½ T. apple cider vinegar
2½ T. sugar
2 T. soy sauce
1 t. cornstarch, dissolved in ¼ c.
water

Combine pork, scallion, salt, egg, and 1 T. cornstarch. Stir in one direction. Stir in ¼ c. water, a few drops at a time, until mixture is sticky.

Heat oil to medium-high temperature. Pick up a handful of meatball mixture. Squeeze mixture through index finger and thumb. Scoop up 1 teaspoonful and drop into oil. Scoop out meatballs as they turn slightly brown and rise to top of oil, and add new ones to pot until all are done. Cool to room temperature.

Reheat oil to high temperature, return meatballs to oil, and deep-fry for a second time, until meatballs turn darker brown (about ½ minute). Scoop out and drain on paper towels.

Remove oil except 2 T. from pot. Brown garlic ½ minute. Add pepper and pineapple, and stir-fry for 2 minutes. Stir in remaining ingredients. Add meatballs, mix well, cover, and simmer 15 minutes.

SWEET AND SOUR PORK

Serves 4

Four ¾-inch-thick center-cut
    porkchops, boned, cut into about
    ¾-inch cubes
2 T. soy sauce
2 T. dry white wine
1 T. cornstarch
½ c. flour
1 qt. vegetable oil or enough to
    cover bottom of pan to 2 inches
2 scallions, cut into 1-inch lengths
1 t. minced ginger root or ½ t.
    ginger powder

1 large green pepper, cut into
    1-inch squares
3 slices canned pineapple, each
    cut into 16 pieces
2 T. cider vinegar
¼ c. sugar
¼ c. ketchup
½ t. salt
1 T. cornstarch, dissolved in ¼ c.
    water

Marinate pork in soy sauce, wine, and 1 T. cornstarch for 1 hour, or overnight in refrigerator, then place in plastic bag. Add flour. Shake until pork pieces are coated with flour. Discard excess flour.

In deep pot, heat oil to medium-high temperature. Deep-fry pork until light brown. Drain.

Reheat oil to high temperature. Deep-fry pork a second time until golden brown. Drain and place in warm dish.

Remove oil, except 2 T. Heat oil to high temperature. Brown scallions and ginger for about 10 seconds. Add pepper and pineapple. Stir-fry for another 10 seconds.

Stir in remaining ingredients. Cook until sauce thickens. Pour over cooked pork and serve immediately.

SWEET AND SOUR SPARERIBS, SHANGHAI STYLE

Serves 8

2–2½ lb. pork spareribs (Chinese style preferred)
¼ c. soy sauce
2 T. dry white wine
½ c. vegetable oil
3 scallions, cut into 1½-inch lengths

½ t. minced ginger root or ⅓ t. ginger powder
3 T. sugar
3 T. cider vinegar
1 T. cornstarch

Have butcher cut across the bones to make three sections, then cut spareribs between bones to make about 24 bone-in pieces. Marinate in soy sauce and wine for 1 hour, or overnight in refrigerator.

Heat deep pot to medium-high temperature. Add oil, heat for ½ minute, and brown spareribs, a few at a time (1½ minutes on each side). Remove from pot. Set aside.

Brown scallions and ginger about 15 seconds, return spareribs to pot, and stir in remaining ingredients. Bring to a boil. Lower temperature and simmer, covered, over medium heat for about 15 minutes, or until meat is tender. Stir occasionally while cooking.

Poultry and Eggs

CHICKEN AND CASHEWS

Serves 4

¾ lb. boneless, skinned chicken
  breast, trimmed
3 T. soy sauce
2 T. dry white wine
1 t. cornstarch
¼ c. vegetable oil
2 scallions, cut into ½-inch pieces
1 t. minced ginger root or ½ t.
  ginger powder

1 large green pepper, cut into
  ½-by-½-inch pieces
½ T. minced hot red pepper
  (optional)
1 T. Hoisin sauce or 1 t. sugar
  mixed with 1 T. soy sauce and
  1 T. flour
½ c. roasted cashews

Cut chicken into ½-inch cubes. Marinate for ½ hour in 2 T. soy
sauce, wine, and cornstarch.

Heat deep pot to high temperature. Add oil and heat until smoking hot. Quick-fry chicken for about 1½ minutes (or until meat
turns color). Scoop up and set aside.

Brown scallions and ginger for a few seconds. Add green pepper
and red pepper if you wish. Stir-fry for a few seconds. Push vegetables to side of pot. Brown Hoisin sauce or sugar, soy sauce, and
flour mixture for about 5 seconds. Stir in 1 T. soy sauce. Turn off
heat. On warm stove, mix chicken with vegetables.

Pour chicken and vegetables onto serving platter. Arrange
cashews around mixture just before serving.

EGG FU YONG

Serves 4

Fu yong is the Chinese name for one kind of hibiscus plant. Egg Fu Yong is named after its beautiful flower.

½ lb. large cleaned shrimp, or crab meat, or lobster meat
½ t. salt
½ t. garlic powder
2 T. dry white wine
2 t. cornstarch
vegetable oil

1 large ripe tomato, cut into 8 pieces
3 scallions, cut into 1-inch lengths
½ t. minced ginger root or ⅓ t. ginger powder
4 large eggs, slightly beaten with ½ t. salt

Marinate seafood ½ hour in salt, garlic powder, wine, and cornstarch.

Heat deep pot to high temperature. Add ¼ c. oil. Heat until smoking hot. Stir in seafood. Quick-fry about 1 minute. Scoop up seafood and set aside.

Return pot to medium-high heat. Add tomato. Stir and cook until tender (about 2 minutes). Add scallions and ginger. Cook another minute.

Two ways for the final touch:

For tender, juicier results, pour egg mixture into pot. Very gently stir and cook until egg is just set. Add seafood. Mix and serve hot.

For an omelet, add seafood to pot. Mix well with tomato. Remove pot from heat. Heat a clean frying pan to medium-high temperature. Add 2 T. vegetable oil. Heat until very hot. Pour in egg mixture to make an omelet. When bottom of omelet is set, spread seafood mixture over it. Lower heat to medium. Cover and simmer for 5 minutes, or until egg is cooked. Flip omelet into serving dish. Cut into 4 pie-shaped pieces.

FAST-STEWED CHICKEN

Serves 4

Serve this chicken with juice over hot cooked rice or mashed potatoes.

3 T. vegetable oil
2 scallions, cut into 1-inch lengths
1 t. minced ginger root or ½ t.
    ginger powder
2 cloves garlic, crushed
1½ lb. chicken legs or wing and
    breast section, cut into
    2-by-2-inch pieces

1 t. minced hot red pepper
    (optional)
1 t. black pepper
1 t. salt
2 T. soy sauce

Heat deep pot to high temperature. Add oil. Brown scallions, ginger, and garlic. Brown chicken pieces until they change color.

Add remaining ingredients and ½ c. boiling water. Cover and bring to a boil. Lower heat to medium-high and cook 15 minutes, shaking pot with lid on every 5 minutes. Skim off excess oil, and serve.

FLAVORED EGGS

Serves 8–12

These eggs can be prepared ahead of time and served hot or cold.

TEA EGGS

12 large eggs
2 whole anise or 2 t. five-fragrance
    spice powder

3 tea bags or 2 T. black tea
2 T. salt

Hard-boil eggs, and crack with back of spoon lightly while still warm. (Be sure not to separate shell from egg.)

Put eggs, anise or spice powder, and tea in 4-qt. saucepan. Add 1¼ qt. water and salt. Bring water to a boil, lower heat, cover, and simmer 1½ hours. Discard tea and anise.

To serve hot, heat juice. To serve cold, remove eggs from juice and refrigerate.

SALTED EGGS

½ lb. salt

12 eggs, at room temperature

Bring 3 qt. water to a boil. Stir salt into water until it dissolves. Cool *thoroughly*.

Carefully place eggs in a deep container or large jar. Add salt water to submerge eggs. Cover. Mark date. Keep in cool place (45–70°). Eggs will be ready in about 3 weeks to 1½ months, depending on room temperature.

Hard-boil salted eggs the same as you would fresh ones and serve hot or cold.

POT-ROASTED EGGS

In a formal Chinese dinner, a cold platter made with pot-roasted eggs, sliced roast beef, roast pork, sweet and sour shrimp is often served as a first course, to go with drinks.

6 eggs

pot-roasted pork shoulder (see
   p. 71)

Hard-boil eggs, shell, and slash 4 horizontal lines halfway through egg white.

Add eggs to pot-roasted pork shoulder during last hour of cooking.

To serve, quarter eggs while still warm, and serve with some juice from pot roast; or chill eggs in refrigerator, quarter, and serve.

GOLDEN-BROWNED CHICKEN FILLET

Serves 4

4 small chicken fillets (total
    1¼–1½ lb.) or 4 chicken thighs,
    skinned and boned
2 T. soy sauce
2 T. dry white wine
⅓ t. salt

2 large eggs
¼ c. flour
1 qt. vegetable oil (or enough to
    cover bottom of pan to 2 inches)
2 c. bread crumbs

Pound chicken with side of heavy knife, or rolling pin, to flatten and loosen texture of meat.

Combine soy sauce, wine, and salt, and marinate chicken for 2 hours, or overnight in refrigerator.

Beat eggs and flour with electric mixer at medium speed for 2 minutes.

In electric frying pan, heat oil to 400°. Dip chicken in batter, then coat with bread crumbs. Deep-fry until golden brown (allow 8–10 minutes on each side; lower temperature if chicken browns too fast). Drain on paper towels and serve hot.

JELLIED CHICKEN MOLD

Serves 8–10

This can be made ahead of time and served for a summer dinner.

1 chicken (2½–3 lb.), boned and
    chopped into about 1-inch
    cubes, skin and all
½ lb. pork rind
3 scallions
3 thin slices ginger root or 1 t.
    ginger powder

¼ c. soy sauce
2 T. dry white wine
½ T. sugar
1 c. cooked diced carrots and peas
⅓ t. salt

Put chicken, pork, scallions, ginger, soy sauce, wine, and sugar in pressure cooker. Add 2 c. water. Cook under 10 lb. pressure for 45 minutes. (If regular saucepan is used, simmer ingredients for 2–2½ hours, or until chicken is very tender.) Cool and release pressure.

Return pressure cooker to medium-high heat. Stir and boil uncovered 10–15 minutes, or until juice thickens to 1 cup. Discard scallions, ginger, and pork.

Mix carrots and peas with salt. Cool to room temperature.

Spread vegetables on bottom of large bowl or jelly mold. Pour chicken, juice and all, over vegetables. Refrigerate 2–3 hours or overnight. Unmold on cold platter before serving.

PEPPERCORN CHICKEN PARTS

Serves 4

Peppercorn chicken tastes delicious hot or cold—it is especially good for picnics!

1 T. salt
1 t. brown or black peppercorns

4 pieces chicken parts (breast and wing sections or leg and thigh sections), rinsed and dried on paper towels

In small saucepan over medium-high heat, toast salt and peppercorns until salt turns light brown and smells good (about 5 minutes). Shake pan occasionally.

Rub salt-pepper mixture, while still warm, over chicken parts. Place in double plastic bags. Tie opening. Refrigerate 1–2 days.

Heat oven to 300°. Place chicken, skin side up, on rack in roasting pan. Cover and roast 1¼–1½ hours.

Remove cover. Turn oven to 450° and roast another 15 minutes, or until skin turns golden brown.

QUICK-FRIED CHICKEN STRIPS

Serves 4

¾ lb. boned, skinless chicken
    breasts, trimmed
⁵/₆ t. salt
2 T. dry white wine
1 large egg white
2 t. cornstarch
⅓ c. vegetable oil
2 garlic cloves, crushed

3 scallions, cut into 1½-inch strips
1 t. minced ginger root or ½ t.
    ginger powder
1 t. minced hot red pepper
    (optional)
1 large green pepper, thinly
    shredded

Fillet each chicken piece into three layers. Cut lengthwise in half; then cut across the grain into thin strips.

Marinate chicken for ½ hour in ½ t. salt, wine, egg white, and cornstarch.

Heat deep pot to high temperature, add oil, heat until smoking hot, and stir in chicken. With brisk movement of chopsticks or a fork, quick-fry and separate chicken strips while cooking until meat changes color (about 1 minute). Remove pot from heat and stir and cook chicken in hot oil for another ½ minute. Scoop up chicken and set aside.

Return pot to heat. Brown garlic, scallions, ginger, and red pepper for about 10 seconds. Stir in green pepper and remaining salt. Return chicken to pot and mix well.

ROAST DUCK—PEKING STYLE

Serves 8–10

Serve with double-layer pancakes (see p. 106) as part of main course.

4¼–4½-lb. duckling
1 t. honey, dissolved in ⅓ c. water
½ loaf bread
1 large onion, peeled
8 six-inch double-layer pancakes (see p. 106)

8 scallions, white part only, cut lengthwise into strips
½ c. Hoisin sauce or 2 T. flour mixed with 2½ c. soy sauce, 1 T. sugar, 1 t. onion powder, ⅓ c. water, and cooked into paste

Defrost duck if necessary, rinse, and dry. Run heavy cord around and under wings and hang suspended overnight to air-dry. Brush duck skin with honey solution 3–4 hours before roasting time.

Heat oven to 350°. Wet bread with water and line slices evenly on bottom of roasting pan to prevent spattering. Place roasting rack on top of bread.

Stuff onion into stomach of duck to keep meat moist. Place duck, breast down, on rack. Roast for about 1¼ hours. Turn duck breast up. Roast another 50 minutes to 1 hour, or until skin is golden brown and crisp. Pour excess grease from pan 2 to 3 times while roasting. Prick skin with carving fork during last 10 minutes of roasting, to let out grease.

To serve: Make slanted slashes on each side of breast in order to get eight 1-inch-wide pieces of duck meat with skin on. Open pancake two-thirds of way. Place one piece of duck and a few scallion strips in opening. Spread ½ t. Hoisin sauce or flour paste over stuffing. Roll up pancake. Eat from hand. With kitchen scissors, cut remainder of duck into 1-by-1-inch pieces and eat as it is.

ROAST DUCK—SIMPLIFIED

Serves 4-6

In some parts of China, when serving duck, the tail is faced toward the honored guest, who has first choice of this prized mouthful.

4½–5-lb. duckling	½ c. Hoisin sauce or 2 T. flour
1 T. salt	mixed with 2½ c. soy sauce, 1
1 t. black pepper	T. sugar, 1 t. onion powder, ⅓
1 large onion	c. water, and cooked into paste

Defrost duck, if necessary, and rub salt and pepper inside and out of it. Run heavy cord around and under wings, and hang overnight to air-dry.

Heat oven to 350°. Peel onion and stuff into duck cavity. Place duck, breast down, on rack in roaster. Roast for 1¼ hours. Turn breast up, and roast another 1–1¼ hours, or until skin is crisp to the touch of fingernail.

To serve: With kitchen scissors, cut off wings and drumsticks at the joint. With breast up, cut along sides of duck to separate back from breast. Split back portion lengthwise into halves, then cut each into 4–5 pieces. Arrange in center of platter. Split breast portion into 2 parts. Cut each into 4–5 pieces. Arrange on top of back pieces. Place wings and drumsticks along sides, to restore duck shape. Serve with Hoisin sauce or flour mixture as a dip.

SAUTEED CHICKEN GIZZARDS AND LIVERS

Serves 4

1 lb. chicken gizzards and livers,
  trimmed, rinsed, and dried
3 T. soy sauce
2 t. cornstarch
2 T. dry white wine
¼ c. vegetable oil
1 large onion, cut into small
  pieces

3 scallions, cut into 1-inch lengths
1½ t. minced ginger root or 1 t.
  ginger powder
3 garlic cloves, crushed
¼ c. bamboo shoot slices
8 water chestnuts, sliced
1 t. cornstarch, dissolved in ¼ c.
  water and pinch of salt

Cut gizzards and liver into ¼-inch-thick slices. Marinate with soy sauce, 2 t. cornstarch, and wine for ½ hour.

Heat deep pot to high temperature. Add oil. Heat until smoking hot. Stir in gizzards and liver. Quick-fry until they change color (about ½ minute). Scoop up and set aside.

Brown onion for 1 minute. Add scallions, ginger, garlic, and cook a few more seconds. Add bamboo shoots and water chestnuts. Stir. Cover and cook for about ½ minute.

Stir in cornstarch mixture and cook until sauce thickens. Remove pot from heat. Stir in gizzards and liver and serve hot.

STEAMED EGG CUSTARD AND SHRIMP

Serves 4

½ lb. medium-size cleaned shrimp
3 large eggs, slightly beaten
1 c. ground pork
1¼ t. salt

1 t. onion powder
½ t. white or black pepper
¼ t. sesame oil or ½ t. salad oil

Spread shrimp on bottom of 8-inch aluminum or foil pan.

Beat eggs and mix with pork, salt, onion powder, and 2 c. water. Pour mixture gently into pan so as not to disturb shrimp.

Steam over boiling water for 20 minutes, or until custard is set. (There will be a few tablespoons of water on top.)

Sprinkle pepper and oil over custard before serving.

STEWED CHICKEN WITH WINE

Serves 4

Serve this hot with juice over cooked rice.

2 T. vegetable oil

6 thin slices ginger root or 2 t. ginger powder

2-lb. whole chicken cut into 2-by-3-inch pieces, dried on paper towel

⅔ c. dry white wine

1½ t. salt

Heat deep pot to high temperature. Add oil. Brown ginger for a few seconds. Add chicken. Stir until all turns color. Add wine, salt, and ½ c. boiling water. Cover. Bring to a boil. Turn heat to medium and simmer for ½ hour. Shake pot with cover on occasionally while simmering.

Turn heat to high. Stir and cook a few minutes more, until sauce thickens and cooks down to about ⅓ cup.

TURKEY ROLL

Serves 16–20

Prepare this ahead of time to serve as cold cuts.

6-lb. turkey breast

3 T. salt

1 t. brown or black peppercorns

Remove turkey bones with a sharp knife and a pair of kitchen shears. Be sure to keep meat and skin in a whole piece. Dry with paper towels.

In small saucepan over medium-high temperature, dry-roast salt and pepper until salt turns light brown and smells good (about 5 minutes). Shake pan occasionally while roasting.

Rub warm pepper-salt all over turkey breast. Roll up turkey with skin on the outside, and tie with cord. Refrigerate overnight.

Heat oven to 450°. Place turkey roll in enamel roaster, covered. (If regular roasting pan is used, cover turkey roll with a piece of foil shaped as a tent. Allow 15 to 30 minutes longer roasting time.) Roast for 15 minutes. Lower temperature to 300°. Roast for 1¼–1½ hours (or until juices come out clear when roll is poked in center).

Cool and refrigerate roll at least 4 hours. Slice thin and serve cold.

TWICE-COOKED CHICKEN

Serves 4–6

2–2½-lb. whole chicken	6–7 garlic cloves, crushed
¼ c. vegetable oil	2 t. salt

Bring 2 qt. water to a boil. Put in chicken. Bring to another boil. Turn off heat, cover, and let pot stay on warm stove for 10 minutes. Remove chicken from water, cook, and cut into about 1-inch cubes.

Heat deep pot to high temperature. Add oil. Brown garlic until light brown. Add chicken. Quick-fry for about 1 minute. Stir in salt. Mix well. Serve either hot or cold.

Seafood

DEEP-FRIED OYSTERS

Serves 4 as main dish; 8 as appetizer

2 large eggs
¼ t. baking soda
¼ t. baking powder
¼ c. cornstarch
¾ c. flour
1 t. salt

1 T. chopped scallions or 1 t. onion powder
¾ lb. shelled fresh oysters, rinsed, drained well, larger ones halved
1 qt. vegetable oil (or enough to cover bottom of pot to 1½ inches)

Beat eggs, baking soda, baking powder, cornstarch, flour, salt, and scallions or onion powder with electric mixer, or by hand, until well blended. Add oysters. Mix well. Set aside for 10 minutes.

In medium-size pan, heat oil to high temperature. Drop 1 rounded tablespoonful of oyster mixture at a time into oil. Fry until golden brown (2–3 minutes on each side). Drain on paper towels. Serve hot.

GOLDEN BROWN SHRIMP AND CABBAGE PATTIES

Serves 4 as main dish; 8 as appetizer

Serve these patties plain or with soy sauce.

¾ lb. small cleaned shrimp
⅔ c. shredded cabbage
¼ c. shredded onion
¼ c. shredded carrots
2 scallions, chopped

2 large eggs
⅔ c. flour
1 t. salt
⅔ c. vegetable oil

Combine all ingredients except oil with 2 T. water. Mix well and let stand for ½ hour.

Heat frying pan to medium-high temperature (375°). Add oil. Swirl to cover bottom of pan.

Drop 1 heaping tablespoonful of patty mixture into pan. Flatten with spoon into a round patty ½ inch thick and 1½ inches in diameter. Fry until golden brown. Turn and brown other side (takes about 8 minutes). Repeat until all are cooked.

LOBSTER CANTONESE

Serves 4–6

1½–2-lb. live lobster
¼ c. vegetable oil
2 scallions, cut into 1-inch lengths
1½ t. minced ginger root or ⅔ t.
   ginger powder

½ c. chopped or ground pork
1 t. salt
1 large egg white
2 T. cornstarch, dissolved in 1 c.
   water

Brush lobster clean under cold water, then precook it in one of two ways: either steam it over boiling water for 20 minutes or bring 2 qt. water, with 2 t. salt, to a boil, place lobster, head down first, into water, cover, and boil for 20 minutes. Drain. Remove lobster's head. Chop claws and tail into 1-inch lengths (with shell on).

Heat deep pot to high temperature. Add oil. Heat until smoking hot. Brown scallions and ginger for a few seconds.

Mix pork, salt, and egg white, and stir it into pot. Quick-fry until meat changes color. Stir in cornstarch mix. Cook until sauce thickens.

Add lobster pieces. Gently mix and cook a few more seconds. Cover and turn off heat. Keep pot on warm stove for 1 more minute before serving to give sauce a chance to soak into lobster meat.

QUICK-FRIED SHRIMP AND HAM

Serves 4

8 oz. medium-size cleaned shrimp
1 t. salt
1 T. cornstarch
1 T. dry white wine
¼ c. vegetable oil

2 cloves garlic, crushed, remove skin
½ c. diced cooked ham
½ lb. fresh green beans, cut into ½-inch lengths

Marinate shrimp for 15 minutes in ½ t. salt, cornstarch, and wine.

Heat deep pot to high temperature. Add oil. Heat until smoking hot. Stir in shrimp and quick-fry until shrimp changes color and curls up (less than 1 minute). Scoop up shrimp and set aside.

Brown garlic until it turns golden brown. Stir in ham and quick-fry for a few seconds. Add beans. Stir-fry for 2 minutes or so. Add ½ t. salt and ¼ c. water. Cover and simmer until beans are tender but still green (about 3 minutes).

Spread contents of pot, juice and all, on bottom of serving dish. Top with shrimp.

SHRIMP AND VEGETABLES

Serves 4–6

¾ lb. large cleaned shrimp
salt
2 T. dry white wine
1 egg white
1 T. cornstarch
1 small carrot, cut into
  ¼-inch-thick slanted slices
1 large broccoli, stem peeled, cut
  lengthwise into 6–8 parts, then
  crosswise into 1-inch pieces

1 piece bamboo shoot, cut into
  similar size as carrot (about ½
  c. sliced)
¼ c. vegetable oil
2 scallions, cut into 1-inch lengths
1 t. minced ginger root or ½ t.
  ginger powder
2 t. cornstarch and ¼ t. salt,
  dissolved in ½ c. water

With flat side of knife, pat shrimp to flatten each piece. Marinate for ½ hour in ¾ t. salt, wine, egg white, and 1 T. cornstarch.

Bring 1 qt. water, with 2 t. salt, to a boil. Add carrot. Boil 1 minute. Add broccoli and bamboo shoot. Bring to another boil. Drain. Set aside.

Heat deep pot to high temperature. Add oil. Heat until smoking hot. Brown scallions and ginger for about 5 seconds. Stir in shrimp. Quick-fry until they change color (about 2 minutes). Stir in cornstarch mixture. Pour in cooked vegetables. Stir and cook until sauce thickens (less than 1 minute).

SAUTEED SHRIMP

Serves 4 as main dish; 8 as appetizer

1 lb. medium-size shrimp in shells
2½ T. soy sauce
3 cloves garlic, peeled and
  chopped

1 T. sherry or dry white wine
½ t. sugar
½ c. oil

Slit shrimp back to three-fourths of length, head to tail, about ¼ inch deep; devein, rinse, and drain well. Marinate shrimp 10–15 minutes in soy sauce, garlic, wine, and sugar.

In deep pot, heat oil to high temperature. With perforated spoon, scoop up shrimp from marinade. Set marinade aside. Add shrimp to oil. Cook about 2 minutes (until two-thirds of shrimp turn color and curl up a little).

Mix marinade with equal amount of water. Stir into shrimp mixture. Cover pot and simmer over medium heat for 3 minutes. Eat as a finger food, hot or cold.

SCALLOP PANCAKES

Serves 4 as main dish; 8 as appetizer

Serve these pancakes plain or with soy sauce.

1 lb. fresh scallops
3 large eggs
1 t. salt
¼ c. chopped scallions

1 t. minced ginger root or ½ t.
  ginger powder
¾ c. flour
½ c. vegetable oil

Rinse scallops, drain well, and slice each across the grain into 4 pieces. Mix well with eggs, salt, scallions, and ginger. Stir in flour, ¼ c. at a time, until well blended.

Heat frying pan to medium-high temperature (or 375° on electric frying pan). Add oil. Heat for 10–12 seconds. Gently drop heaping tablespoonfuls of mixture into pan. Flatten into about 1½ inches in diameter by ½ inch thick—potato pancake size. Brown each side 2–2½ minutes.

SHRIMP AND SWEET PEAS

Serves 4

9 oz. small cleaned shrimp
⅔ t. salt
2 T. dry white wine
1 T. cornstarch
½ t. garlic powder
1 egg white
¼ c. vegetable oil

2–3 scallions, cut into ½-inch lengths
10-oz. pkg. frozen peas, slightly defrosted
1 T. cornstarch, dissolved in ¼ c. water
1 c. dry-roasted peanuts

Marinate shrimp for ½ hour in salt, wine, cornstarch, garlic powder, and egg white.

Heat deep pot to high temperature. Add oil. Heat until smoking hot. Brown scallions for a few seconds. Stir in shrimp (marinade and all). Stir-fry until shrimp changes color (about 1 minute). Scoop up and set aside.

Pour peas into pot. Quick-fry for about ½ minute. Stir in cornstarch mixture. Cover and simmer over medium heat 2 minutes.

Spread contents of pot over bottom of warm serving dish. Top with cooked shrimp. Sprinkle peanuts around edge of dish right before serving.

SHRIMP CANTONESE

Serves 4

¾ lb. large shrimp in shells
¼ c. vegetable oil
3 scallions, cut into 1-inch lengths
1 t. minced ginger root or ½ t.
  ginger powder

½ c. ground pork
1 large egg
1¼ t. salt
2 T. dry white wine
1 T. cornstarch

Slit shrimp back to three-fourths of length, head to tail, about ¼ inch deep, and devein. Rinse and drain well.

Heat deep pot to high temperature. Add oil. Heat for a few seconds. Stir-fry shrimp until half changes color (about 1 minute). Add scallions and ginger. Stir-fry for a few seconds. Push shrimp and all to side of pot.

Combine pork, egg, ¼ t. salt, and wine, and stir mixture into middle of pot. Cook, stirring, for about 10 seconds. Blend together with shrimp.

Add cornstarch mixed with 1 t. salt and 1½ c. water. Mix well. Lower heat to medium. Cover and simmer 3 minutes, stirring twice while cooking.

SHRIMP SHISH KEBAB

Serves 8

¼ c. soy sauce
¾ c. dry white wine
2 t. sugar
1 t. minced ginger root or ½ t.
  ginger powder

1¼ lb. large or medium cleaned
  shrimp
½ lb. bacon, cut crosswise into 4
1 pint cherry tomatoes

Combine soy sauce, wine, sugar, and ginger. Bring to a boil. Cool to room temperature.

Marinate shrimp in cooled sauce for 10 minutes. Scoop up shrimp and save sauce.

Wrap each shrimp in a piece of bacon. Run bamboo skewer through bacon and shrimp, alternating with tomatoes until 5–6 shrimp are on each skewer.

Barbecue, holding 6 inches over medium-high charcoal heat, 3 minutes on one side. Turn and brown another 3 minutes, or until bacon turns brown and shrimp curls up.

STEAMED CRAB

Chinese people associate crab with autumn, when the female crabs are loaded with roe. Steamed crabs are usually enjoyed in the garden, under the full moon and around blooming mums.

Like lobster and clam, crab must be cooked alive. If the lady of the house has a weak stomach, give the gentleman of the house a chance to show his masculinity.

To distinguish a female crab from a male: the shell over the stomach of a female is heart-shaped, while the male's is pointed. Come to think of it, is that the reason females are inclined to be more romantic?

Serve steamed crab as a snack between meals or at midnight. Some soft music and good wine will enhance your pleasure.

How many to buy: Plan 2–3 live crabs per person.

To clean: Hold crab with a pair of tongs and brush clean under running water.

To prepare dip (serving 4):   Combine ¼ c. cider vinegar with 2 t. minced ginger root or 1 t. ginger powder. For a variation, add 1 T. soy sauce.

To cook crabs: Steam over boiling water for 25 minutes. Remove steamer from heat and keep crabs warm in steamer.

To serve: ˙ Place a portion of dip in small dish or wine glass for each person. Provide some nutcrackers and small forks. Place steamer on table, or pick up one crab per person at a time.

To eat: Place crab, stomach side up, in plate. Lift up center shell from pointed end and enjoy the roe, if crab is a female. Turn

crab over. Lift up back shell (apply a little force when necessary), and pull out claws and legs. Crack claw with nutcracker.
Most white meats are locked in the two side chambers. Crack
them and enjoy each bite, with or without dip.

VEGETABLES
AND SALADS

BACON-FLAVORED SPINACH

Serves 4

2 T. vegetable oil
2 slices bacon, cut into 1-inch
  lengths
2 garlic cloves, crushed

10-oz. pkg. fresh spinach, rinsed,
  drained, broken crosswise in
  halves
⅓ t. salt

Heat deep pot to high temperature. Add oil. Brown bacon until crispy.

Brown garlic until it smells good. Put in spinach and stir-fry until it turns color and shrinks to half its original size (less than 1 minute). Remove pan from heat. Stir in salt.

CENTERPIECE SALAD WITH GELATIN NOODLES

Serves 6–8

1 envelope (¼ oz.) unflavored
  gelatin
12–14 radishes, cleaned
salt
2 T. sugar
2 slim, firm cucumbers (about 7
  inches long)

1 T. cider vinegar
1 garlic clove, minced
1 t. black pepper
¼ t. sesame oil or 1 t. salad oil
4 crisp lettuce leaves

To make gelatin noodles: Dissolve gelatin in ½ c. cold water. Stir in ½ c. boiling water. Continue stirring until gelatin is completely dissolved. Pour into a plastic sandwich container or any small square container. Chill to jell. Dip container in hot water for a few seconds. Unmold. Cut into 1½-inch noodle-size strips. Cut radishes in halves, and marinate in 1 t. salt and sugar for at least 1 hour (for best results, overnight in refrigerator). Drain.

Partially pare cucumbers, split lengthwise in halves, remove seeds, then slice crosswise at angle into ⅛-inch slices (or slice with grater).

Marinate slices with salt for 1 hour; then drain well.

Combine vinegar, garlic, pepper, and oil. Mix well with cucumbers.

Line bottom of serving dish with lettuce. Top with cucumbers and dressing. Spread gelatin noodles on top, then cover with radishes. Chill before serving.

CHINESE CABBAGE IN CREAM SAUCE

Serves 4–6

2 T. vegetable oil	⅔ t. salt
3 slices bacon, cut into 1-inch lengths	¼ c. milk
	1 T. cornstarch
1 garlic clove, crushed	½ t. sugar
1–1¼ lb. Chinese cabbage hearts quartered lengthwise and cut crosswise into 2 parts	1 c. chicken broth

Heat deep pot to high temperature. Add oil. Heat for a few seconds. Brown bacon until crisp. Brown garlic for a few seconds. Stir in cabbage and quick-fry until soft (8–10 minutes). Add salt. Mix well. Scoop up cabbage and set aside.

Pour remaining ingredients into pot. Stir to blend, then bring to a boil. Lower heat to medium. Stir and cook until sauce thickens (about 2 minutes).

Return cabbage to pot. Mix well with sauce. Cover and simmer 2–3 minutes, or until cabbage is tender.

FAST-STEWED EGGPLANT

Serves 4

¼ c. vegetable oil
4 slices bacon, cut into 1-inch lengths
4–5 garlic cloves, crushed

3–4 slim, firm eggplants (about 1¼ lb.), cut into bite-size triangles
3 T. soy sauce
1 t. sugar

Heat deep pot to high temperature, add oil, heat for a few seconds, and brown bacon until crispy.

Add garlic. Brown for a few seconds. Add eggplant. Stir and cook for about 3 minutes.

Stir in soy sauce, sugar, and ½ c. water. Cover, bring to a boil, and lower heat to medium. Simmer, stirring occasionally, 10–12 minutes, or until eggplant is soft to the touch.

PICKLED CABBAGE

Fresh, serves 4; "ripe," serves 8

½ head cabbage (about ¾ lb.), broken into roughly 1½-by-1½-inch pieces
1 small carrot, diced
1 stalk celery, cut into ½-inch lengths

3–5 cloves garlic, peeled
1 T. minced hot red pepper
½ t. brown or black peppercorns
½ t. MSG (optional)
3 t. salt

Rinse a grease-free qt. jar with boiling water. Cool to room temperature.

Divide cabbage into two parts. Put half into jar, add rest of ingredients, then squeeze remaining cabbage into jar.

Add water up to neck of jar. Screw cover on tightly. Turn jar upside down and shake vigorously for 2 minutes, or longer. Unscrew cover. Press down cabbage, and add more water to cover. Screw on cap tightly. Shake sideways for a few minutes. Mark date on lid, *and do not open jar before maturing time.*

For fresh-tasting pickled cabbage, keep at room temperature for 2 days. Serve chilled as salad. For sour-tasting cabbage, allow 7 days. Refrigerate once jar is opened.

(To reuse pickle juice, strain liquid, discard contents of strainer, and add more seasonings and salt to taste, following directions above. Cabbage will be ready 2–3 days sooner with reused juice.)

QUICK-FRIED BROCCOLI

Serves 4–6

2 T. vegetable oil
3 slices bacon, cut into 1-inch
  lengths
2 garlic cloves, crushed

2 large broccoli, stems peeled,
  quartered lengthwise, then cut
  into 1½-inch lengths
⅔ t. salt

Heat deep pot to high temperature. Add oil, heat for a few seconds, and brown bacon until crisp. Brown garlic for a few seconds.

Stir in broccoli. Quick-fry until it changes color (about 2 minutes). Cover and simmer over medium heat about 3 minutes (longer if softer broccoli is preferred).

QUICK-FRIED CHINESE CABBAGE

Serves 4

1 T. vegetable oil
2–3 slices bacon, cut into 1½-inch
   pieces
½ t. minced ginger root or 2
  garlic cloves, crushed

1–1¼ lb. Chinese cabbage, cut into
  1½-inch lengths
¾ t. salt

Heat deep pot to high temperature, add oil, and heat for a few seconds. Brown bacon until crisp. Add ginger or garlic, and heat for a few seconds.

Stir in cabbage and quick-fry until cabbage changes color slightly (2–3 minutes). Stir in salt. Cover and simmer over medium heat 3–4 minutes (longer if softer vegetable is desired).

QUICK-FRIED STRING BEANS

Serves 4–6

3 T. vegetable oil

3 slices bacon, cut into 1½-inch
lengths

2–3 garlic cloves, crushed

1 lb. fresh string beans, cleaned
and snapped in half

2½ T. soy sauce

1 t. sugar

Heat deep pot to high temperature, heat oil for a few seconds, and lower heat to medium-high. Brown bacon until crisp.

Add garlic and brown for 10 seconds. Stir in beans. Quick-fry for about 2 minutes, or until beans turn dark green. Add soy sauce, sugar, and ¼ c. water. Cover and simmer 8–10 minutes, or until beans are tender.

SHREDDED CABBAGE SALAD

Serves 4–6

¾ lb. cabbage (tender,
ivory-colored part preferred),
finely shredded

⅔ t. salt

1 clove garlic, minced

⅔ t. black pepper

¼ t. sesame oil

Mix cabbage with salt. Let stand at room temperature for ½ hour. Squeeze slightly to get rid of juice. Mix in garlic and pepper until well blended. Mix in sesame oil. Chill before serving.

VEGETABLE SALAD

Serves 8

12–14 radishes, cleaned
2 t. salt
3 T. sugar
2 cucumbers, partially pared, seeded, and cut into ½-inch cubes
2 stalks celery, cut into ½-inch cubes

1 green pepper, cut into ½-inch squares
1 clove garlic, minced
2 T. vinegar
½ t. black pepper
½ t. sesame oil

Marinate radishes in 1 t. salt and 2 T. sugar for at least 1 hour (for best results, overnight in refrigerator). Drain.

Mix cucumber, celery, and green pepper with 1 t. salt. Let stand for ½ hour. Pour out juice. Add garlic, vinegar, 1 T. sugar, and black pepper. Mix well and chill for at least 15 minutes.

Pour salad into serving dish. Decorate with radishes and sprinkle with oil.

STARCHES

ABOUT RICE

Basically, four kinds of rice for Chinese cooking are found in supermarkets: rice which needs no rinsing includes enriched long grain and enriched short grain; rice which needs rinsing to remove pumice includes plain long grain and plain short grain.

Usually 1½ cups rice need 2½ cups water or enough to cover 1 inch over rice. It is advisable to use less water than too much. You can always add a bit more water and simmer a little bit longer when rice becomes dry.

One cup long-grain rice makes 3 cups cooked. One cup short-grain rice makes 2½ cups cooked. In other words, short grain is less absorbent and therefore needs less water.

How to Cook Rice: Place 2 c. enriched short-grain rice in a heavy-bottom medium-size saucepan. It is very important to use the right size pan for the amount of rice. For example, for 2–4 c. rice, use medium-size saucepan; for 4–6 c. rice, use 4-qt. pan.

Add water to cover 1 inch over rice. Bring to a rolling boil. Stir thoroughly once. Cover.

Reduce heat to medium and simmer 15 minutes. Turn off heat and keep pan on warm burner another 10 minutes.

Remove pan from stove. Fluff rice lightly with chopsticks or fork.

How to Reheat Cooked Rice: You can steam rice over boiling water for 15 minutes (allow 30 minutes if rice is frozen). Or you can heat frying pan to medium-high temperature. Add 2 T. vegetable oil. Swirl to cover bottom of pan. Add rice and ¼ c. water. Cover and simmer until water evaporates (about 10 minutes). Sprinkle with a little salt, if preferred.

The two following recipes show ways to use cooked rice.

FRIED RICE

Serves 4

5 T. vegetable oil	2 c. cooked rice
1 medium onion, cut into strips	½ t. salt
2 scallions, cut into 1-inch lengths	2 eggs, slightly beaten with ¼ t.
¼ lb. smoked pork butt or spicy	salt
cold cuts, cut into 1½-inch-long	2 T. soy sauce
thin strips	
1 large green pepper, cut into	
strips	

Heat frying pan to high temperature. Add 3 T. oil, and heat until smoking hot. Brown onion and scallions. Stir in meat and cook for ½ minute.

Add green pepper and cook for a few seconds. Stir in rice and salt. Cook for another minute.

Push rice mixture to side of pan. Pour 2 T. oil in center of pan. Heat oil a few seconds, pour in egg mixture, cook a few seconds, then slowly mix all ingredients together. Add soy sauce. Stir until well combined.

FANCY FRIED RICE

Serves 6–8

You can substitute lean pork, chicken fillet, or shrimp for the flank steak in this recipe.

¾ lb. flank steak
4 T. soy sauce
1 T. cornstarch
2 T. dry white wine
⅓ t. sugar
6 T. vegetable oil
2 large eggs, slightly beaten with
 ¼ t. salt
4 scallions, cut into 1-inch lengths

1 t. minced ginger root or ½ t.
 ginger powder
1 small carrot, cut into thin slices
¼ c. thinly sliced bamboo shoots
3–4 dry mushrooms, softened in
 warm water, stems removed,
 caps sliced, or ¼ lb. fresh
 mushrooms, sliced
3 c. cooked rice
⅓ t. salt

Slit meat in half lengthwise, then cut against the grain into ¼-inch-thick pieces. Marinate for ½ hour in 2 T. soy sauce, cornstarch, wine, and sugar.

Heat deep pot to medium-high temperature. Add 3 T. oil. Heat for a few seconds. Pour in egg mixture and make an omelet. Turn once. Remove from pot. Cool. Cut into pieces of a size similar to beef pieces.

Add 3 T. oil to pot. Heat over high temperature until smoking hot. Stir in beef. Quick-fry until three-fourths of beef changes color. Scoop up beef. Set aside.

Brown scallions and ginger about ½ minute. Stir in carrot, bamboo shoots, and mushrooms. Quick-fry another ½ minute. Scoop up vegetables. Set aside.

Stir rice into pot. Lower heat to medium high. Stir and cook until rice is thoroughly heated. Stir in salt and 2 T. soy sauce. Blend in all cooked ingredients.

CHINESE PANCAKES

Serves 4

These pancakes may be served hot with or without jams or jellies.

½ c. flour
1 c. milk or water
2 large eggs
⅓ t. salt

1 scallion, finely chopped, or ½ t. onion powder
4½ T. vegetable oil

Combine flour, milk or water, eggs, and salt. Beat until smooth. Stir in scallion or onion powder.

Heat 10-inch fry pan to medium-high temperature. Add 1 T. oil. Swirl to coat bottom of pan. Heat oil for a few seconds. (For next 7 pancakes use only ½ T. oil for each.) Slowly pour 2 T. batter into pan, swirling pan to spread a thin layer over surface. Heat until edge of pancake shows light brown and separates from edge of pan. Turn and brown other side.

HOMEMADE PANCAKES AND SKINS FOR EGG ROLLS, SPRING ROLLS, WONTONS, FRIED NOODLES, AND SUI-MAI DUMPLINGS

DOUBLE-LAYER PANCAKES

Makes 12 pancakes

In northern China, spring is welcomed with double-layer pancakes stuffed with Mu-hsu pork, beef and bean sprouts, or other favored quick-fried dishes. Spring rolls, as these pancakes are called, go so well with Peking duck that most people would not think of eating duck without pancakes.

Making the pancakes involves a bit of work, but the joy of eating them makes all the effort worthwhile. They can be stored in refrigerator 3–4 days, or much longer in plastic bag in freezer. When ready to use, steam over boiling water for 15 minutes, or 30 minutes if frozen.

3 c. flour

5 T. vegetable oil

Place flour in deep bowl. Slowly stir in 1½ c. boiling water. Mix well with chopsticks or fork until cool enough to handle. Flour your hands. Knead dough slightly in the bowl to form a ball. Cover and let stand for 45 minutes.

On floured surface, gently knead dough until smooth. Divide dough into 24 pieces. Roll each piece into a ball, then press with hand into size of a half-dollar coin.

Place oil in shallow dish, and dip one side of each dough piece in it. Then top each with an ungreased dough piece.

Heat electric frying pan to medium temperature (300–325°). To bake pancake on stove, use heavy-duty frying pan for even heat distribution.

With rolling pin, roll one double-layer dough piece into a 6-inch-diameter pancake. Place on ungreased frying pan and cook, with cover on, for about 1 minute (or until big air bubbles form between the layers). Lift top layer of pancake two-thirds of way while still hot (once cold it will be difficult to separate the 2 layers). Keep in covered dish.

EGG ROLL SKINS—SHANGHAI STYLE *Makes 28–30 skins*

4 c. flour

½ t. salt

Mix flour and salt well with 2 c. water. Refrigerate overnight.

Heat a non-Teflon electric fryer to 275°. (To keep fryer steady, spread damp towel over tabletop. Place fryer on towel.)

Place bowl of batter inside large bowl of ice. Batter is workable only if kept cold. Scoop up a handful of batter. Palm up, tilt hand slightly away from you and extend fingers, so batter runs over end of fingers. Flip fingers to palm, to give elasticity to dough. Constant flipping keeps the batter workable.

Lightly touch fryer with batter (in your hand) in a swirling motion, to leave about a 7-inch-diameter skin. Quickly collect batter into hand, then, using batter in hand, snatch up excess batter from baking skin. Mend small holes with dabs of batter on index finger. Bake until edges turn up (35–40 seconds). Lift skin gently and place on plate.

Wipe fryer with dry towel after removing each skin. After making 3 or 4 skins, when batter becomes sloppy, return batter to chilled bowl and take up another handful of chilled batter.

To store skins, separate them and let cool to room temperature before storing flat in plastic bags. Refrigerate if used within 3 days, or freeze up to 3 months. Defrost before using.

SPRING ROLL SKINS IN A JIFFY   *Makes 30–32 skins*

This recipe calls for an electric crêpemaker.

2 c. flour   2 large eggs
½ t. salt

Preheat electric crêpemaker.

Blend flour, salt, and eggs until smooth. Pour a portion of batter into dipping pan. When indicator light starts fluctuating on and off, dip the heated pan (domed side down) into batter. Lift up and turn over (domed side up), placing back on heatproof surface. When underside of crêpe turns light brown, turn crêpe pan upside down over a plate. The crêpe should fall off automatically with the touch of a fork. There is no need to reheat the pan. Just keep going until you have 30–32 spring roll skins made in a very short time.

SKINS FOR EGG ROLLS, WONTONS, FRIED NOODLES,
AND SUI-MAI DUMPLINGS   *Serves 8*

2 c. flour
1 large egg

To make egg roll skins, with chopsticks or fork, stir ½ c. boiling
water into flour, a few tablespoonfuls at a time. Mix egg in until
roughly blended. Squeeze into a ball. Cover with wet paper towel
and let stand for 1 hour.

On floured board, knead half the dough until smooth. Fold and
press a few times to form a square. With rolling pin, roll dough into
a ¹/₁₆-inch-thick skin. Sprinkle flour over and under dough while
rolling. Cut skin into six 6½-inch squares. Repeat with remaining
dough, to make a total of 12 egg roll skins.

To make wonton skins, repeat above procedure, but cut each
dough half into 3¼-inch squares, to make a total of 64 squares.

To make fried noodles, pile up 5–6 layers of egg roll skins. Sprinkle
flour between layers, fold in half, and cut into thin strips. Shake
loose.

Deep-fry in 400° oil 4–5 minutes, until noodles turn golden
brown. Sprinkle salt to taste.

To make sui-mai dumpling skins, on slightly floured board, knead
half the dough until smooth. Fold and press a few times to form an
oblong shape.

With rolling pin, roll dough into ⅛-inch-thick skin. Sprinkle
flour over and under dough while rolling.

Cut skin lengthwise into 4 equal parts, then crosswise into 5
equal parts, making 20 skins. Repeat with second half.

STEAMED BUNS

Makes 20 buns

4 c. flour
2 T. vegetable shortening
¼ c. sugar

1 pkg. (¼ oz.) active dry yeast,
dissolved in 1½ c. warm water

Place flour, vegetable oil, and sugar in bowl. Stir in yeast mixture, a couple of tablespoonfuls at a time. Mix with chopsticks or fork until well blended. Squeeze and knead into a ball. Cover bowl with plastic wrap. Allow dough to rise to double in size (2½–3 hours at 70–72°).

On floured board, knead dough with *controlled strength* (press halfway down to mix) for about 10 minutes. Cut dough in half. Roll and stretch each half to form a 15-inch roll. Sprinkle more flour over dough, then cut each half into 10 even pieces. Place each piece on a 2-inch wax paper square. Let buns stand at room temperature for 30 minutes or longer, until double in size.

Place buns with wax paper in steamer, making sure they are 1 inch apart. Steam over boiling water for 15 minutes. Remove immediately from steamer. Remove wax paper while still hot. Serve in place of rice.

TO MAKE STUFFED BUNS

1 recipe raised dough (preceding)
2 c. finely chopped Chinese or
  regular cabbage
¾ t. salt
¾ lb. ground pork

3 scallions, chopped
½ t. minced ginger root or ¼ t.
  ginger powder
2 T. soy sauce
2 T. oil

Prepare and divide dough into 20 pieces, as for steamed buns. Roll each piece between palms of hands to form a ball, then press palms together to squeeze ball into a disk. With rolling pin, on floured board, roll disk into 3-inch-diameter skin.

Mix Chinese cabbage with salt. Let stand at room temperature for 20 minutes. Squeeze out juice. Mix well with remaining ingredients and 3 T. water.

Place 1 rounded tablespoonful of cabbage stuffing in center of skin. Pinch pleat so that all the edges come to top center and pastry is round with a swirl design on top.

To cook, you can steam or fry:

Steaming: Place each pastry on a 3-inch wax paper square. Arrange pastries on wax paper in steamer at least 1 inch apart. Steam over boiling water for 15 minutes. Remove pastries from steamer immediately. Remove wax paper while still hot.

Frying: Heat electric fryer to 400°. Add 3 T. vegetable oil. Swirl to coat bottom of pan. Heat oil until hot. Loosely arrange pastries, 10 at a time, to form a circle. Brown bottom of pastry for 1 minute. Lower heat to medium high. Add ½ c. water. Cover and cook until water dries completely (about 10 minutes). Serve plain or with soy sauce as a dip.

STIR-FRIED NOODLES

Serves 4–6

This dish makes a good lunch to go with a light soup. It is also popular in buffet dinners. Smoked ham can be substituted by any spicy cold cuts or leftover meat.

6 T. vegetable oil

2 eggs, slightly beaten with ¼ t. salt

2 scallions, cut into 1-inch lengths

1 t. minced ginger root or ½ t. ginger powder

5 dry mushrooms, softened in warm water, stems removed, and caps cut into strips

⅓ c. bamboo shoot strips

¼ lb. cooked smoked ham, cut into strips

½ lb. cooked, drained egg noodles

½ t. salt

2 T. soy sauce

Heat frying pan to high temperature. Add 2 T. oil. Pour egg mixture into pan and make a thin omelet. Cool. Cut into strips. Set aside.

Return pan to stove. Add 4 T. oil. Heat for a few seconds. Brown scallions and ginger. Add mushrooms and bamboo shoots. Stir-fry for about 1 minute. Add ham. Cook another minute.

Stir in noodles. Add salt. Mix and cook for another minute. Splash soy sauce evenly over noodle mixture. Add egg strips. Stir and cook until well blended.

DESSERTS

Fresh fruits in season are usually served as dessert after dinner in Chinese meals. The following recipes are used for more or less special occasions.

ALMOND COOKIES

Makes 24

¾ c. butter or margarine, softened
¾ c. sugar
1 large egg
3 t. almond extract
1½ c. flour

½ t. baking soda
¼ t. salt
24 blanched whole almonds
1 egg yolk, beaten slightly with 1
    T. water

With electric mixer at medium speed, beat butter or margarine, sugar, egg, and almond extract until very light and fluffy (about 4 minutes).

Sift flour, soda, and salt together. Beat into butter mixture until well combined. Refrigerate at least 1 hour.

Divide dough into 24 equal parts. Gently form each into a ball. Refrigerate.

Heat oven to 350°. Lightly grease 3 cookie sheets. Place 8 balls 2 inches apart on 1 sheet (keep the rest refrigerated). Gently flatten each to ¼-inch thickness. Press 1 almond into the center of each.

Brush with egg yolk mixture. Bake 15 minutes, or until light golden color. Remove sheet from oven; let cool 10 minutes before removing from cookie sheet with pancake turner.

Prepare another sheet while one is baking.

ALMOND-FLAVORED CHAMPAGNE CUP

Serves 4

1 envelope (¼ oz.) unflavored
    gelatin
½ c. cold milk
½ c. hot milk

½ t. almond extract
11-oz. can mixed fruit cocktail
4 candied cherries

Dissolve gelatin in cold milk. Mix well. Stir in hot milk until gelatin is completely dissolved. Stir in almond extract.

Divide fruit cocktail, juice and all, among 4 champagne glasses. Pour almond mixture over fruit. Place glasses in refrigerator and chill until firm. Top with candied cherry.

ALMOND DELIGHT

Serves 8

2 envelopes (¼ oz. each)
    unflavored gelatin
1 c. cold milk
1 c. hot milk

2 t. almond extract
20-oz. can seedless litchis (or any
    favored canned fruit)
11-oz. can mandarin orange
    segments

Dissolve gelatin in cold milk. Stir in hot milk. Add almond extract. Stir well and pour into an ice cube tray. Refrigerate until set (3–4 hours), and cut into small cubes.

Combine with fruit, juices and all, in large bowl. Add 2 c. cold water and 8 ice cubes. Serve as a refreshing dessert.

CANDIED BANANAS

Serves 6–8

¾ c. flour
1 large egg
½ c. milk
2 medium-size firm, ripe bananas

1 qt. vegetable oil (or enough to cover bottom of pan to 2½ inches)
3 T. vegetable oil
1 c. sugar

Beat flour, egg, and milk with mixer on medium speed for 3 minutes (or beat by hand until well blended).

Peel bananas. Cut each into 6 pieces.

Heat 1 qt. oil to medium-high temperature (375°).

Dip banana pieces, a few at a time, into batter. Deep-fry until light brown. Drain and set aside. (Save frying oil for later use.)

Heat pan to medium-high temperature. Add 3 T. oil. Stir and cook sugar until chopstick or a wooden spoon touches bottom of pan without making the grating sound that sugar crystals make. Remove pan from heat. Lower burner to warm temperature. Return pan to burner to keep syrup from hardening.

Heat frying oil to high temperature (a cube of white bread browns immediately when dropped into oil). Return cooked bananas to oil to brown a second time (1 minute). Drain. Carefully drop a few pieces at a time into syrup. With chopsticks or tongs, pick up glazed banana pieces, one at a time, and dip each into a bowl of ice water. Then place on a lightly greased platter and serve immediately.

GOLDEN COINS

Serves 8–10

For substitute of stuffing mixture given in recipe use ½ c. fa-vored jam mixed with 1½ T. flour and 2 T. finely chopped wal-nuts.

½ c. sweetened red bean paste
1½ T. vegetable oil
¼ t. sesame oil (optional)

2 cylinders buttermilk or
country-style biscuits

Combine bean paste and oils, and mix until well blended.

On floured board, flatten biscuit with palm of hand. Roll and turn biscuit to form a round "skin" about 2 inches in diameter, with center thicker than the edge.

Place 1 t. stuffing in center of each skin. Pinch and gather edges together and seal. Place stuffed biscuits, pinched side down, on floured board. Press with fingertips until each is about ⅓ inch thick all round.

Follow one of the following procedures to cook biscuits:

TO BROWN
¼ c. vegetable oil

Heat fryer to medium-high temperature (350–375°). Add 2 T. oil. Swirl to coat bottom evenly. Lower heat to medium (300°). Turn and brown biscuits, 10 at a time, until both sides turn golden brown (allow 8–10 minutes—if biscuits brown faster, lower heat). Press lightly while browning, and add oil as needed.

TO BAKE
1 large egg yolk, blended with 1
   T. water and ¼ t. salt

Brush top side of biscuits with egg yolk mixture. Bake as directed on biscuit wrapping.

SESAME CRISP

Makes about 24 cookies

This cookie is especially made for our Dragonboat Festival, May 5 of the Chinese calendar, in memory of a patriotic poet, Ch'u P'ing, who lived during the period of contending states (around 403–221 B.C.).

As a poet, he won the emperor's favor but was later dismissed from his official advisory position when the wayward emperor opposed his suggestions. Overcome with worry and sorrow for his country, Ch'u P'ing drowned himself. To this day we celebrate his fame by racing dragonboats and eating sesame crisp and sweet rice wrapped in bamboo leaves.

Instead of sesame seeds, you might substitute dry-roasted sunflower seeds, finely crushed walnuts, or crushed almonds.

1 c. flour	1 large egg
½ c. sugar	1 qt. vegetable oil (or enough to
¼ c. dry-roasted sesame seeds	cover bottom of pot to 2 inches)

Mix flour, sugar, sesame seeds, and egg with 2–3 t. cold water (depending on the humidity of the room—dough should be fairly dry). With one hand, squeeze and knead hard, to get dough ingredients together.

On a well-floured board, knead dough into a ball. Then, with rolling pin, roll dough into ⅛-inch-thick pancake. Cut pancake into rectangles 1 by 2 inches. Make a ⅔-inch slash in the center of each rectangle. Push one end through slash and straighten out into a bow tie.

Heat oil to medium high. Deep-fry bow ties until golden brown. Drain on paper towel. Cool to room temperature before storing. Stored *tightly covered* at room temperature, these cookies can keep for months.

SHERBET AND MANDARIN ORANGES

Serves 4

1 qt. orange sherbet (or other favored flavor)

11-oz. can mandarin oranges, drained, chilled

4 t. grenadine syrup

4 T. whipped cream

4 candied cherries

Divide sherbet among 4 stemmed glasses or dessert dishes. Arrange orange slices on top. Pour syrup over each. Top with whipped cream. Place 1 cherry on top of each. Serve immediately.

Index